REASONS
Beyond
MYSELF

MY INSPIRATIONAL JOURNEY
FROM LIVING ON THE STREETS
TO PROTECTING THEM

BRION SIMS-JOHNSON

First published by Brion Sims Johnson 2021

Copyright © 2021 by Brion Sims Johnson

Website: brionsimsjohnson.com

This book reflects the author's recollections of past events, people, places, and experiences. Some names and identifying information has been changed to protect their privacy.

Paperback ISBN: 978-1-7373874-0-4

eBook ISBN: 978-1-7373874-1-1

First Edition

Editing by Laura Silverman

Proofreading by Anja Schmidt

Cover art by Michael Rehder

Interior Design by Veronica Scott

CONTENTS

INTRODUCTION

In life, we all dream about being successful. Sometimes we're not given the best starting position in life to start our journeys towards success, but we all have to start somewhere. Where I'm from, that window of opportunity to achieve success becomes even smaller for people that want to make it out. Daily struggle is rooted into every move that you want to make. Bills seem like they become impossible to pay, eviction notices become the norm, living with different family members becomes insurance, and struggling day to day seems like a never-ending cycle.

Unfortunately, I fell under the long list of names of people born into this cycle. I was one of those people who weren't dealt the best hand to start the game called "life." My family fell under the category of poverty. Living in projects, living in bad neighborhoods, and living on government assistance became the playing cards that started my game in life. I felt trapped growing up—this was my life and there weren't many alternatives to it. The neighborhoods I lived in didn't give much room for people to improve themselves. They felt more like encampments rather than a place to live and one day call home.

Not too many people can say that they have made it out of that type of lifestyle. We call that lifestyle "the mud." That's when you go through the dirt and grime in life to get to where you want to be. It's a constant struggle to make things work, which makes the pathway to success more difficult to reach. Success seems like a long shot when you're born somewhere that offers limited opportunities to be successful.

If chances and opportunities are so few in this type of environment, then why am I here? How did I break the cycle? How did I make it out? There's not a day that goes by when these questions don't run through my head. I promise every question will be answered in this book. My journey will shed light on everything that seems to be a mystery at this point. This is my opportunity to share with you a journey that stems from the roots of a struggle. My story is one of many ups and downs in life that eventually led to a better place.

Fortunately, life is different for me now. I wake up every morning with an opposite hand than the one I was dealt. Every day before work, I get up and I put on my uniform. My uniform comes fit with a badge. Yes, a badge. I'm a police officer. For some people, getting dressed for work is just a normal task, but for me, it's more of a lifestyle. Every day I put on my uniform, every night I make an impact, every day I eat a meal, and every day I return home at the end of my shift serves as a blessing and a reminder to me. It serves as a reminder of how far I've come in life because I remember when these essentials weren't a part of my life. Every morning it feels like

I'm living in a dream world. My job is a part of this dream world. My job provides me with the opportunity to have more in life. I'm frequently asked by curious minds why I do the job I do? A person of my background usually doesn't pick the career field I have chosen for my life. They say people from my neighborhood are supposed to despise cops so why did I become one? I promise this too will be answered in this book.

* * *

Before we get into my job, I want to tell you a little about the man behind the badge. I am much more than my badge, the job I have or the things I own. Yes, I make arrests, I direct traffic, I change lives, but my life began long before I ever put on a badge. My story extends much further than my badge will ever show you. Life brought me many challenges that molded me into the man I am today. I had to struggle and fight through the mud to be where I am right now. I had to break the cycle.

The basis of why I do what I do stems from who I am inside. I don't feel as though I chose this career. My life journey led me to this point. God molded me into the man I am today. I always prayed to God to be a wise man, and I feel that everything I experienced throughout my lifetime made me into the man I prayed to be. God gave me this gift, but he also gave me a unique backstory to mold me into that man. Everything isn't created overnight. It's a journey.

God created a path for me in life, and I used all of the strength and courage I possessed to walk that path. I tell some people what I've been through to get here and they're left in a state of disbelief. I've had people stare at me and say, "I bet you had it easy growing up. Just look at your life." One could assume that I've always had a good life based on my current position in life now. They have no idea that I journeyed through the "mud" to get here, but people tend to assume a lot about me. They assume I'm from Texas, they assume I grew up with a well put together family and they assume that I've wanted to be a cop my whole life. Their assumptions of me are far from the truth. My journey in life was very unique and guided me to this point. I don't like for people to assume my journey in life, so instead, I'll tell you.

In order to fully understand this journey and who I am now, I gotta take you back...ALL the way back. We have to venture back to the beginning of my journey towards success. I have to take you back to a point in my life before the badge, before the new city, before my new way of life, before my dream was even a thought. I challenge you to read this book in its entirety and try to understand my upbringing in life up to this point. The basis of every question asked so far is rooted into the person I am inside. My journey in life allowed me to become this man. Everyone in life has a journey. Everyone has a road they've travelled to be here. This is mine.

CHAPTER 1:

INITIAL BACKGROUND

My name is Brion Cortez Sims-Johnson. For those who have never formally met me, my name is Brion (bree-AWN) not "Brian," but strangers who call me by my first name never seem to pronounce it the correct way. To the common world I was Brion, but to my family I was simply known as Cortez. My family and the local neighborhood felt that Cortez had a better ring to it, so I was rarely called by my first name.

I was born in East Saint Louis, Illinois in a neighborhood known as Washington Park, but my first memories are from a small country town known as Lebanon, Illinois. I spent most of my later childhood days establishing memories from East Saint Louis, IL and on the south side of Saint Louis, Missouri.

I was raised by a single black mother with two kids. My mother often times worked two jobs to cover all of the expenses in the household, but it never seemed to be enough at the end of the month. Since my mother struggled paying the bills, we were constantly moving around and staying with different friends and family members. We frequently ventured to different churches to receive food donations. We slept in church vans in the parking lot and various homeless shelters when homes weren't available for us. These living arrangements were only during the rough times, which seemed to cycle every few months for us.

We definitely didn't have the best life, but my mother always tried to give us the best life that she could. We always lived in bad neighborhoods, but my mom tried her best to make us feel like we weren't living in the so-called "hood."

When we endured these rough times in life, my mother always tried to transform them into something positive in my head. My mother became so good at transforming these negative experiences into positive thoughts that I didn't even realize that we were poor. When we picked up donated boxes of food from the church, my mother always tried to point out the good snacks that she knew I'd liked so that I wouldn't focus on the "donation" part of it. When we slept in the van that was parked in the church parking lot, she'd try to make it feel as more of an adventure rather than a dirty old van that we had to sleep in. When we stayed in bad areas and shelter homes, we would constantly hear yelling, cursing and continuous gun shots coming from outside in the streets throughout the night. My mother would just hold me tight and tell me to sing one of my favorite songs until I eventually fell asleep. I didn't realize the sad reality of the situations until I was an adult and reflected back on everything.

Despite the bad times, my mother always tried her best to ensure our happiness. When we didn't have gifts for Christmas, my mother worked overtime back to back until she was able to purchase gifts for us. When everyone in the neighborhood was out celebrating on the 4th of July, my mother returned home with a big bag of fireworks for us to go celebrate too. My mother even surprised me with a bright red St. Louis Cardinals baseball shirt one day after school, which immediately became my favorite shirt in my closet. She made me feel as though we were the richest in my cloud of thoughts. She made us feel like we were truly winning in life when in reality we were in a downward spiral.

I don't blame my mother for this. Being a single mom with two kids wasn't an easy task. My mother gave birth to my brother when she was just 15 years old. She had me just five years later, so she was still fairly young herself.

Since our fathers weren't present in our lives, my mother had to assume both roles of a mother and a father. I never knew my father, because he never wanted to be a part of my life. My dad left when I was born and didn't come back. Growing up, I always asked my mom about my dad and even hoped he'd return back to my life one day, but he never did.

My mother was left alone to raise two kids by herself at a young age. She had no other option but to be strong for her children. It was just me and my older brother.

My big brother's name is Justin Sims, but everyone in the neighborhood called him J-Rock. He was the first to be born out of my grandmother's grandkids, and he was well loved by our entire family, including our extended family. My brother was very respected in St. Louis. He wasn't much of the bullying type, but he earned his respect from the mental and physical strength that he possessed.

At 17 years old, Justin had a stocky, athletic build, and looked like a grown man. He took full responsibility for his role as a big brother and as the eldest grandchild. Justin vowed that he'd always defend our family no matter what. In my eyes, he was fearless. He was my protector.

Then there was me. I grew up as a strange kid, but I mean "strange" as in unique. As I mentioned, I was initially raised in the small town of Lebanon, Illinois, so I saw the world as a small place with country vibes. This small town of Lebanon was the only place for me. I had a lot of friends, and everyone in the neighborhood pretty much knew each other. I lived a very sheltered life in this small town, but that all changed when my mother decided to move to St. Louis, Missouri because times got hard.

My mother was low on funds, and she thought the big city would offer more opportunities for us. The city was actually worse for us. St. Louis changed my entire life, and it showed me a whole new side of the world that I had no idea about at the time. Drugs, violence, gangs, street rules and many others threats posed a challenge for us growing up in the St. Louis environment.

We bounced around a lot to different homes in St. Louis, and we could never keep a place for a long period of time. My mom struggled every month to pay the bills, and the eviction notices on the outside of our door became the new norm for us. We eventually found a place to live in St. Louis, and my mom enrolled me in Froebel Elementary School.

I was a smart kid, and a huge nerd. My accent was different from all of the other kids in my neighborhood and at my school, because I had moved from the country to the big city. My "foreign accent" caused the other kids in the school to question me and my origins.

I was never a bad kid in school, but I had a smart mouth. As a kid, I felt that I should have the last word in just about everything that was said to me. My teachers surely didn't find this amusing, and my mother definitely didn't find it "cute." My mother constantly had to come pick me up from school, due to me getting in trouble for saying something that I shouldn't have said to a teacher or another student. Either my mother got a call from the school telling her how brilliant I was and recommending gifted schools, or they were telling her that I was mouthing off again and having tantrums in class. My mother always thought that was funny. She told me that "tantrums" weren't for kids like me.

Even though my mouth got me into a ton of trouble, my mom never whooped or spanked me. She didn't believe in physically disciplining her children. She attempted to whoop me one time in my entire life, but she felt bad about it afterwards, so she decided that talking to me would work best. My mother's friends always critique her parenting skills for not physically disciplining me. They told her that I needed my butt spanked, but my mom never gave in to their ideas about how she should discipline me.

She always told me, "You're not a bad kid. You just need to control your mouth." She added, "I can't punish you for that since I know where you got it from, but you still need to control it."

Then she would just smile at me, and I'd smile back.

Times got hard in life, so my mother and I had to move to a homeless shelter in Alton, Illinois. This was a memory my mother had wanted me to never be able to recall in life, but I remember it clear as day. My brother had gone to live with a family member, because he was too old to stay in the shelter with us. My mother wanted us to be together, but if my brother had come with us to the shelter, he would've been forced to stay in the adult men's side of the shelter. My mother felt that would've been unsafe for him.

I went to a different elementary school during this time, and the kids there constantly teased me because I lived in a homeless shelter. Everyday they would call me names like "homeless boy" or something in relation to being homeless or staying in the shelter.

The teasing was nothing new to me. As I said before, I was a weird kid. Growing up, I never really felt like I fit in with any group. I was lost. I just stayed inside playing videogames, listening to music and reading books all day, because of the lack of friendship.

I never really had friends after I left Lebanon. No one liked me. I honestly don't know why. They just didn't like me. I was always labeled as different and bullied for it.

Bullying was a constant throughout my childhood. I was bullied and teased by the white and the black kids. I got bullied on multiple levels. I was bullied for living in a homeless shelter. Girls called me ugly behind my back, but the girls also took time to let me know how ugly I was to my face too. I was beat up for being smart and making good grades, because other students hated seeing me excel in the classroom. The black kids at school called me nerd, called me ugly, made fun of my hair and clothes and tried to fight me every second of the day. The white kids at school called my skin color dirty, stinky, and used multiple racial slurs. I heard it all.

Now don't get me wrong, not all of the students were bullying me, but the ones who did it made sure it made a lasting impact on me. The students who were doing the bullying took turns with it. The black kids would make fun of me on the bus, and the white kids would make fun of me at school. I got attacked from all sides throughout the day and constantly had to fight.

Out of all the fights I was involved in throughout my life, I initiated exactly zero of them. My mother enrolled me in Oakville Middle School thinking that it would protect me from the danger of inner-city schools, but it only transformed the "danger" into a new type. It was ironic that the school my mother had sent me to in order to keep me away from bullying and trouble was actually causing the most bullying and giving the most trouble I had ever received.

After school, I would run to my house, cry and ask my mom why no one liked me. She would just hug me and tell me that I was a good kid and that the other kids would eventually see that in me—but they never did.

Even though I struggled to find and connect with friends, I was grateful to have a mother that made me feel better during these times. She provided everything she could for me, and I was definitely a mama's boy. I also had my big brother to rely on.

My big brother would see me sad, punch me in my arm and say, "Keep yo head up boy. Never let your enemies see you with your head down."

My brother's words of encouragement always made me feel stronger and gave me new energy in life. My family was special to me. They were the reason I kept my smile throughout all of the madness in our lives.

Out of all the craziness I experienced in St. Louis, my mother was always there to comfort me at the end of the day, and my brother was always there to make me smile. If anything, they were the ones that kept me sane. They were my rock and stone. No matter how many schools I went to or how many houses and neighborhoods we moved to, one thing stayed consistent—my family. That by itself was good enough for me to be content with my life.

I felt like I had all that I truly needed. I just knew that we'd always be together and nothing would ever separate us. Little did I know, my life was about to change forever.

CHAPTER 2:

FOREVER 12 YEARS OLD

T he year I turned twelve had to be one of the longest years of my life. My birthday celebration consisted of my mother giving me a few kisses, telling me how blessed I am and my brother taking me out for some food. It was a pretty simple day. I had no idea what this year would hold for me, and I had no clue that my years of being a kid would be cut short. I remember this day the clearest.

I had just returned home from another exhausting day at Oakville Middle School, and when I walked in our apartment, all of the furniture was put up. Everything was packed to the fullest in boxes and stacked along the walls. We didn't remodel the apartment very often, so I knew a home makeover wasn't the case. I looked across the room and saw my brother sitting on the couch putting his clothes into a duffle bag. I remember feeling confused about the situation but also excited about a potential move. I was used to moving from place to place, hood to hood, and friend's house to friend's house. In fact, I had lived in over fifty homes in my life, so this wasn't an absolute shock to me. I was excited because I initially thought that we were moving away from our dangerous neighborhood to a better one. This new move would also mean that I could finally leave the school that had been teasing and bullying me for what felt like forever. I wasn't always excited for a new move, but this one felt long overdue.

Confusion quickly replaced my feeling of excitement as I looked around and saw whose items were packed in the apartment. I noticed that my things had already been packed and set aside next to the door, along with my brother's, but my mother's things were kept separately from ours. My suspicion grew as my mother slowly walked towards me with a look as if she needed to tell me something important. I started to think "maybe I did something wrong and now I'm in trouble." I dropped my school backpack down on the ground and waited for my mother's words.

She approached me and said, "Tez, you and your brother are going to go stay with your grandmother for a couple of weeks." After hearing those words, I was relieved to know that I wasn't in trouble. I was also happy that we would all be moving to my grandma's house together. I didn't really like going to my grandma's house by myself, because she was really strict and her house smelled like old people and cigarettes. As long as I had my family with me, I felt like I could tolerate being at my grandma's house for a few weeks.

My eyes searched around the room as I asked my mom, "Where is your stuff?"

Her faced showed signs of internal remorse and absolute pain as she looked me in my eyes. Tears filled her eyes as she uttered the words, "I'm not going with you. I'm going to go somewhere else, but I'll be back to get you in a couple of weeks, ok?"

I only responded with "Ok," as my mom quickly hugged me tighter than she ever had before.

At that very moment, if I had known for a fact that I wouldn't see my mother again for almost three years, I probably would've hugged her a little longer, looked at her for a second more, and kissed her while begging her not to leave...but I didn't know. I had always believed everything she had ever said to me without second guessing her.

Despite my utter confusion, there was someone in the room who wasn't as clueless as I was in that moment—my brother. He was older, knew the world a bit more than I did, and he knew exactly what my mother was going to do next. After hugging my mom, I looked over to the corner of the room, and stared at my brother. His stocky frame then lifted from the couch with his arms crossed and his face stern. His eyes pierced in the direction of my mother from across the room, but he didn't say a word to my mom. He just stared at her.

I trusted my mother's words, so my eyes reflected the opposite of my brother's grim stare. My eyes had a sense of excitement, compassion, with only a little bit of sadness, because I "knew" I'd see my mother again in two weeks. It wouldn't be the first time I was away from her for a few weeks. I felt like I was a "big boy" and that I could handle everything until she returned.

My brother's eyes possessed sadness, pain, and worst of all—betrayal. I didn't realize at that age that my brother always knew more than I did. Neither his eyes nor his heart bought into the words my mother had said to us. He was only seventeen and I was only twelve, but my brother knew he was now going to have a lot more responsibility than he could've ever imagined.

As my mom handed me my duffle bag and gave me one last hug, she kneeled down and said, "You know I love you right?" Then I said with big eyes lit, "I love you too ma." She said the same to my brother, but he didn't bother to stay for idle goodbyes.

He simply walked straight out the door and muttered three simple words—"Yeah, I know."

We lived in St. Louis, Missouri and my grandmother lived in Lebanon, Illinois. The journey to my grandma's house was just a couple of bus rides and a train ride away from us. The train ride to my grandma's house felt unusual that day. My brother absolutely hated going to my grandma's house, because she tended to bad mouth our mom a lot. She also just got on my brother's nerves in general like old people are supposed to do, but this time my brother seemed a little more disturbed than normal. While we were on the train, my brother kept staring out of the window without saying a word.

I sensed that my brother was upset, so I leaned over towards him and said, "Man, what's wrong with you? Mama said she'd be back in two weeks." My brother then turned towards me and looked me straight in the eyes. He had a look on his face as if he wanted to open up and tell me the truth about something, but something else held him back from saying it.

Instead, he simply responded, "Yeah," and then turned back towards the window and continued gazing outside.

When we arrived at my grandmother's house in Lebanon, she greeted us with warm smiles, which me and my brother were never fooled by, but we always gave one back. We unpacked our bags and got ready for our two-week stay at my grandma's house. I wasn't too thrilled to be at her house, but I was happy to be back in town with my old childhood friends. Most of my distant family lived in Lebanon, so it was like a double bonus for me. Returning back to town felt like the right move.

When I returned to town, everyone was shocked by my new hairstyle, which were dreadlocks. Everyone said that they thought my dreads were cool. I felt like my return was already off to a good start based on the hair compliment alone. I didn't have to worry about bullying in Lebanon, because I was back in town around all of my old friends.

I was enrolled in school at Lebanon Middle School. School was simply school—boring, but friends made it worthwhile. I was in seventh grade at the time, and my luck kept changing for the better. Girls in the school used to write the names of two boys that they thought were the cutest in school onto both of their arms. I remember being in 5th period Algebra class, and I saw one of the popular girls in school writing on her arm. I leaned back out of my chair to get a better view of what she was writing, and I saw my name written in big letters on her arm. That made my day. Maybe even my life for awhile. I thought that my life was finally going to start changing for the better. Everything seemed to be on the right track, except for one thing—my mom.

My mother's two-week deadline was rapidly approaching and we still hadn't heard from her. I sat by the window in my grandma's living room every night just thinking about my mom and wondering where she could be. I tried not to think too much about her whereabouts, but I couldn't help but focus on the two-week deadline when she would return. I was always checking the phone and asking my grandmother if my mom had called for me—but there was nothing. We hadn't heard a word from her. I was 12 years old and a huge mama's boy so I couldn't help but worry about her.

While I was busy worrying about my mother, my brother Justin was quickly losing his patience with my grandmother. Justin seemed upset almost every night. He tended to not spend much time at the house because of his feelings towards my grandmother.

In his words, "I love her, but man, she just can't keep her mouth closed for a second."

Anyone who knows my brother knows that those words were said out of as much love as possible. My brother was easily annoyed by a variety of people, and my grandmother was that person at the time. Without my mother present, living with my grandmother became a great challenge in itself. My grandmother would complain to us every single day about how she didn't have any food for all of us and how my mother needed to chip in money, but we didn't have contact with my mother to get her to do anything. My grandmother would always tell us that we needed to do something to get some food in the house, but we were kids. There weren't many legal ways to go about getting food.

Two weeks finally came around, but that's all. Just the date. Not a phone call. Not a knock at the door. Not anything from my mom. This worried me since this was the first time that she had been away for weeks without being in contact with us. I just figured that maybe she meant three weeks instead of two. Three weeks came around and still there was nothing from her. Then I thought "Maybe she just got busy with work and needed to work a couple more weeks." Almost two months went by and still there was nothing. I started thinking of every possibility for the delay in her return. I felt more confused than anything else. I thought to myself, "Well, maybe she couldn't buy the tickets back home and had to find another way back." By three months, my excuses for my mom no longer made sense, and I won't even bother to elaborate on the silly, supernatural excuses I started developing in my head about her delayed return.

I think by "two weeks," my mother was actually referring to the time period my brother would survive living with my grandmother before he snapped. Within a couple of months living with my grandmother, Justin was fed up and had reached his breaking point. The final straw came when my grandmother was literally prepared to fight me because I had used one of her display towels in the bathroom to dry off. My grandmother had about fifty towels in the house and said that they were all off limits and used for different occasions. Before that day, I used my own towel before it got thrown away in the trash. My grandmother got upset about the towels and tried to hit me, but my brother, the protector, didn't allow anyone to lay a finger on me.

He quickly stood in front of my grandmother and said, "You're not touching my brother."

I felt safe standing behind Justin, knowing that he was there to protect and that nothing would happen to me.

My grandmother cursed and swore at him and kept muttering about how I needed to learn my lesson. My brother was a man of respect and felt that respect was something that should be shown and given. He also always took the rap for me. No matter what it was. If I ate one of my grandmother's sandwiches when she said not to eat it, my brother would claim he did it. If I broke one of her CDs, he would say he accidentally broke it. If I broke a window, he would claim he was the one who had done it. In short, he was always there for me.

Justin stepped in front of my grandmother whose heart seemed to jump at the sight of him standing up in front of her. He never disrespected elders and always showed me the proper way to handle these situations. He told her that she didn't have to lay a hand on me to get her point across.

Justin said, "It was a simple mistake. I'll take your towels and go wash them myself if that's what'll make you happy?"

My grandmother almost never dropped an argument. She wanted to initiate physical discipline towards me, but my brother said otherwise. My brother had proved to be the more dominant and mature person at that moment.

My grandmother then stormed down the hallway and yelled, "I'll wash my own freaking towels!" (But with more "French words").

Justin sat me down and said, "Tez, you know how Granny gets about those towels. I know you didn't mean anything by it, but just make sure you don't touch em. This ain't our house. You gotta watch how some people are. She ain't Mama and we ain't her kids. I can't believe she tried to fight you over some towels. Boy, I wish she would've. I would've knocked her face in."

My brother would always say he would knock someone's face in, chest in, or just knock them out in general. You have to understand that Justin is one of the most respectful men and would never intentionally harm or disrespect anyone for no reason, but he was making it known to everyone that "I don't care who you are or where you come from. Mess with my little brother, and something's getting knocked in."

After Justin spoke with me, I just nodded my head and took in his words like I always did. My brother showed me what it meant to truly defend someone you cared about in this world. He stood up to my grandmother and didn't back down. Justin told me that he would never let anything bad happen to me, and I believed him.

My brother told me that my grandmother was getting under his skin. He said that he was sick of my grandma talking crap about our mother and trying to put her hands on me. Even though my grandmother was the one causing most of the issues in the house, Justin felt that his presence was making things worse. He said that he was also sick of her complaining about food, so he had decided to go back to St. Louis.

Justin said, "People really don't want to take care of two kids, so maybe they'll have more sympathy for just a 12-year-old boy rather than a 12-year-old and 17-year-old boy."

My brother felt that by leaving, my grandmother wouldn't stress out so much since she would only have to worry about one kid. Justin told me that he'd keep in contact with me and that things would probably feel different, but I needed to stay strong. My brother told me that he was leaving but that he would always keep his promise—he'd never let anything bad happen to me. Justin then grabbed his bags and left out of the front door. Just like that, the two people I loved the most were out my life. I was now by myself.

When both my mom and brother left, I think it hurt me more because they weren't dead. They were very much alive. I felt like it was of their own freewill not to be around me. I felt like I was back in St. Louis where no one wanted to be around me. I kind of understood why my brother was doing it, but it still didn't make me feel any better. I felt very much alone.

I found out later in life that my brother went back to St. Louis, dropped out of school, and lived amongst his friends and with my mom's older sister, Janet. My brother's actions were just part of his rebellion, because he knew that my mother was not coming back. I believe he was hurt and never really knew how to express that pain. He had an idea of her absence beforehand, but I think it hit him differently when the months passed by and his thoughts about our mom's absence became real.

When I realized that she wasn't coming back, it broke me into pieces. I couldn't believe it. I was heartbroken. I felt betrayed. My excuses for her leaving sounded so stupid when I started to think about it. Even though the truth had hit me, I couldn't completely accept it. A huge part of me still wanted to believe that she was coming back for me. I was still a kid, and I still loved my mom. There was that side of me that still believed that she was coming back everyday, but then there was this other side of me that just wanted to scream and yell in agony. I tried to hide my emotions, but it was an utter failure.

After my brother left, everything started to fall apart. I was greatly affected by losing two important people from my life. My performance in school became poor, I rebelled against everyone, and the once smart kid turned into the dumb kid. When my mom left, I felt distant from everyone in school. I felt like no one understood the pain I had inside of me. She looked me straight in my eyes and lied to me. How could I have believed her? The world didn't make sense to me anymore, and I just felt stupid. That's the best word. Stupid.

Because I felt like this inside, I started to act out in school. I mostly got in trouble for back talking, not doing work or not going to class. The thing that hurt the most was the feeling that no one cared. When the teachers would send me out into the hallway after getting into trouble in class, the teachers never came out to say, "Hey, what's wrong? What's going on in your life right now?" The teacher would come out and escort me to the office, and the office would just give me an after school detention slip or an in school suspension. End of discussion. No questions asked.

With school slowly slipping from my grasp, things only got worse for me. Without my brother with me, there was no defense for me against my grandma's rage.

One morning around 4:30am while I was sleeping on the couch, my grandmother just randomly woke me up screaming at the top of her lungs "Get out of my house!"

I thought there was a fire or something. I was sleeping in my shorts with no shirt or shoes on, and I started panicking. My grandmother was screaming for me to get out of her house and muttering something under her breath about my mother not giving her money. I got up from the couch, and she shoved me out of the door.

I asked her, "Can I at least grab my shirt and shoes?

And she said, "Your stuff will be outside when you get back!"

Back from where? She said it as if I was going on a vacation or something. Then as she shoved me out of the door, literally shoved me outside, all I heard were the locks closing on the inside of the door. Just like that, I was homeless and had to walk barefoot on the cold street pavement, without a shirt, at about four in the morning looking for somewhere else to go.

After walking in circles and brainstorming for about five minutes, I decided to go over to my great uncle's house. He was someone who always seemed to look after my older brother, but I personally didn't have a close relationship with him. He lived about a mile and some change away, but the walk there seemed so much further away since I was traveling without a shirt or shoes. I constantly stepped on rocks, gravel and sharp items the whole journey there. The whole time walking, I thought to myself, "What in the world just happened? What's happening to my life right now?"

I made it to my uncle's house after a long walk across town. Everyone called my uncle "Uncle Jimmy." He had four kids himself and was also taking care of his son's cousin. His oldest son was named Jim Jr but we all called him JJ. JJ's cousin was Floyd. JJ and Floyd were both seniors at Lebanon High School and JJ was only a year older than my brother.

When I first arrived at the house, I was just happy to be around some people who liked my brother. When I told them what my grandmother had just done, they thought that maybe I was lying about the "getting kicked out" part until they went with me to gather my things from my grandmother's house that same day. They soon discovered that everything was scattered about on the pavement in front of her house, as if a windstorm had come through.

We started gathering the small amount of things that I had, which seemed to be a lot due to the scattered appearance. We finally collected all of my things and returned to my uncle's house.

Living with my uncle was different, because I had to adjust to living with a big family, which was new for me. There were eight of us in one household. With six kids in the house and only one bathroom, getting ready for school was very hectic. I had to take really quick showers in the mornings and tried to chip in with chores, but I wasn't very good at it. Living with my uncle was a new and difficult experience, but I didn't have many alternative options. While adjusting to the new living arrangements at my uncle's house, school was still going downhill for me.

When I was in St. Louis, the bullying I experienced mostly came from other kids. This time, it wasn't the kids, but the school administrators who were doing the bullying. I may not recall this woman's name, but I'll never forget her face or the words she uttered to me one day.

After I was sent to the office, one of the office administrators who worked the front desk said to me, "Brion, I really don't know what to do with you right now."

I don't know how she knew, but she heard that I had been kicked out of my grandmother's house.

She proceeded to say, "I want to suspend you, but I know you don't have a place to live so you'd just be on the streets bothering people, and I really don't want to have to deal with you out there so I don't know what to say."

I was shocked. I really didn't know what to say to something like that without getting into trouble again, so I just got up and proceeded to leave. I was used to school administrators saying remarks to me like that and getting away with it. They saw me as another "problem" rather than a kid who was hurting inside.

Another incident with the school administrators occurred a few weeks later. I was in gym class and it was my turn in kickball. When I was getting ready to kick the ball, I heard the gym doors fly open and the principal, Mrs. Donald, stormed into the gym. The pitcher froze in his tracks, dropped the ball and immediately turned towards Mrs. Donald, who seemed beyond upset as if someone had broken into her car or something of that nature. Mrs. Donald waved her finger for me to come over, and I didn't know what to expect. When someone approaches you with that much anger, you start to ask yourself "Hmm, did I do something wrong to this person?" Everyone in gym class was absolutely silent and continuously shifted their eyes from me to Mrs. Donald and back to me again.

Mrs. Donald then approached me with aggression and said, "What are you doing here?!" I was lost and confused at this question.

I simply responded to her "Going to school."

Mrs. Donald then said, "You're not supposed to be here!"

I'm thinking to myself, maybe she's talking about me going to summer school and that there's no need for me to continue going to school for this academic year, but she wasn't referring to that. The kickball game had been paused, and everyone just stood by and continued to stare at us.

Mrs. Donald then escorted me out into the hallway and ordered me to clear out my locker. With each book I took out of my locker, I was asking myself "Is this really happening? Is she really kicking me out of school?" The answer was yes. She was kicking me out of school. Not for behavioral issues, but because I didn't have some medical papers that she stated the school needed. The way she was going about putting me out of school, made me feel like a criminal. I was escorted through the school by administrative staff until they were able to fully clear out all of my belongings from the lockers and classrooms.

The office staff then escorted me outside to the school entrance with the principal, Mrs. Donald, leading the way.

Mrs. Donald then faced me outside and said, "If you come within 200 feet of the school property, I will call the police and you'll be arrested for trespassing on school premises."

I was speechless. I was lost, confused, heartbroken, and dazed by everything that was happening to me. I had just been kicked out of school and told not to come back all because of some medical paperwork. There were guys who got into fights and still had the option to come back, but I was not a fighter nor was I granted access back.

I was only *twelve*. I was always told as a kid that education is the key to a bright future, but that future had just been taken away from me. I tried numerous times to get back into that school, but every option of getting back in school would have required my mother coming back, which was not happening anytime soon.

After being told to leave the school, I wandered around town until I eventually got tired of walking. I sat down on a nearby street curb and thought to myself, "What do I do now?" I had lost my mom, brother, and now school wasn't even in my life anymore. I felt as though life was against me at this point, and it seemed as though I had been dealt a losing hand. As I sat on the curb, I dropped my head down and stared at the ground. At that moment, I just wanted to hear my brother's voice tell me to keep my head up. I wanted to hear my mother tell me to get up and come back home. I wanted these things, but no one came.

Time passed by just as quickly as the cars that sped past me on the street. The night sky took its rightful place for the day, and the streetlights started to flash on. I was stuck in my web of thoughts and had no means of escape. For the first time in life, I felt like there was nothing I could do. I stood up and started making my way back to my uncle's house. I thought to myself that things couldn't possibly get any worse than this, but I couldn't be more wrong.

* * *

Living with Uncle Jimmy quickly became hell. He was a churchgoing man who woke us up every Sunday to go to the local church. He was always in the front of the church and shouting the loudest. In the eyes of a lot of people, Uncle Jimmy was the holiest man around, but I knew a different side of him. He was a good man at times, but he possessed many faces. He would yell at me after church about money and not having anyway to take care of me, a lot like my grandmother had been doing to me. He sounded a lot like her, and I knew what was coming next.

I had been down this road before. I know taking care of a kid is a lot of work and requires money, but he yelled at me as if I was supposed to go stand in the unemployment line and make a difference. Uncle Jimmy would always ask me the same question after church, "Where are you staying tonight? You're not staying with me. I can't take care of you. I don't where you're gonna go." One random day he made it clear to me that I would now have to take care of myself and that I was no longer welcome at his home. Just like that I was on the streets.

Without school, a home, or a family, I just wandered the streets all day. One day, I was so worn out and exhausted that my body just dropped to the ground. I sat on the pavement, and I asked myself, "What am I going to eat? Where am I going to stay? How am I going to get money?"

These were questions for an adult that a 12-year-old child now had to answer in life. I never thought finding a place to stay would be so difficult since I had a lot of family members in that small town of Lebanon, but my innocence of the world around me was quickly broken. When I asked my family members in town if I could stay with them, I received the same response from each of them: they needed money first, they don't have room, or simply that they just don't want to help out. One family member after another turned me down. These were the same family members that would smile at my mother at family functions and say to her that if there was ever a time of crisis, they would be there to help out, but they didn't help me. Once again, I felt stupid to have believed them.

I had no money, and I ran out of clothes. I was left with one dirty outfit to wear around town everyday. News quickly spread around town that I was homeless and wandered the streets all day. People knew this, but no one would help. One night, I slept at the park on the slide, wondering to myself if someone would try to hurt me in my sleep. I was scared, but I didn't have many choices in life to complain. I had to find a way to survive.

One day I laid down on an outdoor bench in front of Dairy Queen. One of my cousins worked there. She was one of my great aunt's daughters. I saw her talk to another woman inside, and then my cousin came outside to talk to me. I was so happy, because in my head, they had seen me outside in need of help and were going to give me some food or something to drink. Yet again, I was wrong.

She came outside to the bench I was laying down on and said, "I'm going to need you to leave this property. We can't have you laying on the benches because those are for customers."

I looked in her eyes and simply said, "I'm sorry, I'll leave."

Another part of my innocence was stolen at that moment. I always thought family had your back, but I was learning that it wasn't always the case.

With sleep locations always in question, I tended to focus on the bigger issue—food and money. I obviously needed money first in order to get food, but my moneymaking ideas didn't come through for me like I initially wanted. I had to resort to other means to get food. I stole food from a local shop in town, because I felt like I was at the point of starvation where I couldn't go another second without food.

One week after I started stealing, a cousin of mine in town had stopped me and told me that my brother was looking for me. They called my brother from their phone and handed it to me. I don't know how my brother found out that I was stealing from the store, but he started to question me about my newly acquired food.

My brother asked, "Where did you get the money to buy the food?"

I was talking to him on the phone, but I could feel his presence as if he was in front of me. I never wanted to keep anything from my brother, so I came clean and told him that I had been stealing food from a store for the past week. I saw my actions as necessary in order to survive.

I argued, "Why should we care about their store? They have more than enough food and don't give a crap about us? They don't care if we live or die, so why should I care about their stuff?"

My brother lowered his voice and simply said, "Because it's not right and it's not what we do."

My cousins were huge thieves. They said they stole because life wasn't giving them anything, so they felt like they had to take it. Justin never applauded their lifestyle nor did he want me to be the same as them. He didn't want me to go down the same road as my cousins. Justin usually had pity on me, but not this time.

He continued, "We don't steal from anyone! You hear me? No one! What's theirs is theirs and that's the way it's gotta be. I don't care how hungry you get man, don't ever steal from nobody."

His words echoed through my head and forced me to look at myself. I was starting to change for the worse. That's not who I wanted to be. I didn't want to transition into a thief. I never wanted to lose myself. After only one week of stealing, my spree had come to an end—forever. I never stole anything from anyone after that day.

I always respected my brother's words and wisdom, and I took them to heart. Hearing the disappointment in his voice was enough for me to never do it again no matter the situation. It's probably the same reason why I never used any drugs in my life. I never wanted my brother to be disappointed in me or my decisions in life. I always respected my brother's words, and they turned into my core values. My brother's words still echo in my head throughout my life.

So instead of stealing, I resorted to doing odd jobs around the neighborhood. One of the jobs I did consisted of helping out the local church. I was always ready to help the church, because they always had some sort of food being served at every event. I helped them burn trash outside of the church, cleaned up, and even got poison ivy from pulling weeds in the area no one else wanted to. I knew there was a possibility of poison ivy where I was working, but I didn't care. I knew people got rewarded for doing things that no one else bothered to do, and I was hoping that if I helped the church, I would hopefully get some type of help in return. Long periods of time passed, and I didn't receive anything for the work I did.

After helping the church for quite awhile, I decided to take a more direct approach to the situation. I went up to the head pastor of the church, Pastor Wilson, who was the husband of my great aunt Brenda (my grandmother's older sister). Aunt Brenda happened to own the church. Pastor Wilson was probably one of the nicest men I have ever met, and he wasn't even my blood uncle. I told him that I had finished everything and to call me if he ever needed help around the church. I paused for a moment afterwards in the hopes that I would be compensated for the work that I did.

But all he said was, "Thank you."

That's it. No food, no clothes, no nothing. At the time, I was only 12 years old and didn't understand the bigger picture. I thought that by helping, I would get an immediate reward, but God had something bigger planned for me.

After weeks of helping Pastor Wilson, I found a greater sense of respect for the job that I was doing for the church. I no longer expected something in return, but I helped because it gave me something to do and kept me away from trouble. There was always something to do at the church, and I got about ten shades darker from constantly being in the sun and working all day. I worked from sunup to sundown. I took pride in the work that I did, and it gave me joy to be useful.

Church was a peaceful place for me. I felt like it was a safe place for me to be, and it provided me with a connection to my faith that I couldn't see at the time. I felt a strong presence, as if someone higher than me was watching me and had my back. The only times my peace was disturbed at church, were the moments when my Uncle Jimmy would be present.

Every day after church service, my Uncle Jimmy would give me his, "Where are you going to live?" speech. Sometimes he would tell me that I could stay with him for a night, but then other times he'd just take off after giving his speech. During the nights that he would actually let me stay, it was just for the nighttime and I had to be out of his house before morning. I was not allowed to use anything at his house or eat any food there. Despite Uncle Jimmy being an unpleasant man, his wife was always very sweet to me. I felt she was the reason he would let me stay on the nights that I was allowed. She snuck me food behind my uncle's back and frequently tried to convince him to let me stay, but his voice always overpowered hers.

I came out of church one night, and I saw my Uncle Jimmy's face in the parking lot. He approached me along with his son JJ, Floyd, and others that I didn't know. As Uncle Jimmy approached me, I was expecting one of his famous "Where are you going to live?" speeches, but this speech was not like any other speech he had ever given to me. Uncle Jimmy went on a 45min rant about how I wasn't going to be anything in life. His speech was about me "facing reality."

He shouted each word at me and said, "You need to face reality! Everyone in your life is gone! No one wants you! Don't you get it? Nobody wants you. Your dad didn't want you! That's why he left you. Your mom didn't want you and that's why she left. Your brother's not here because he didn't want you either! You need to face reality and understand that you're alone! You're by yourself and ain't nobody gonna help you. You need to grow up and be a man."

Uncle Jimmy then took a break from his "face reality" speech and switched to attacking my dreams.

He asked, "What do you want to do in life?"

By this time I was already crying from the first part of his speech, and simply said, "I'm going to be a football player."

He started laughing at me, and the people who were with him started laughing too. They were mocking me, and it was breaking me inside. I felt vulnerable, defenseless and no one was there to protect me. Each word and each face that I saw laughing was a direct hit to me.

After laughing at me, he said, "You suck! How are you gonna be a football player. You ain't even good. You'll never make it! What else do you want to be?"

I then said a basketball player, but I should've known that was going to be his next point of attack towards me.

He then quickly responded, "A basketball player? You suck at that too! There's nothing you're good at and no one wants you."

Bit by bit my self-esteem, along with my innocence, all fled away. I sat there crying and just thinking to myself, "What if he's right? What if my mom, dad and brother all left because they didn't want to be with me? What if no one wants me? He has to be right. I'm not good at anything." I had lost control of my thoughts, and my uncle's words were in the driver's seat imprinting everything in my head.

At that moment, I started thinking to myself, "Does anyone even care that I'm crying right now?" Looking back at it now, no, I don't think they did. It was like my tears just encouraged my uncle to keep throwing insults and attacking me. My uncle didn't offer an apology or anything. His words didn't even have a positive message to them. He was just a man that prided himself on attacking people that were not in a position to fight back. He was a bully. I just stood there frozen and broken. I couldn't do anything but cry. My uncle just continued attacking me, until I got tired of being attacked and started walking away from him.

As I was walking away, my uncle continued yelling at me in the distance saying, "Where are you going to go? No one wants you! No one is going to help you! You need to face reality!"

My uncle's voice didn't fade away until I was far enough down the road where I completely lost sight of him. No matter how far away from my uncle I walked that night, his voice still echoed in my head. I cried myself to sleep that night at the park. I felt completely alone. Throughout a large chunk of my life those words of "No one wants you" hit me, and they stuck for a long time. It was a very long night at the park for me.

Despite the struggles in my life, I continued my work at the church. One day during church service, I sat at the back of the room. I was wearing the same stinky, dirty clothes I had been wearing for a long time. I looked homeless—well, I was. A 12-year-old hobo. I smelled horrible, and I was embarrassed. I sat in the back of the room, awaiting the end of service so that I could start working again. Pastor Wilson was starting to close out his sermon for the day, but then he said something I didn't expect. After Pastor Wilson finished his message, he asked for an offering, but this offering was not for the church.

Pastor Wilson said, "I would like to take one more offering. This one is for brother Cortez. We cannot call ourselves people of the church and ignore someone in need that we see every day. We can't do that."

I was in complete shock. I didn't hear much more after that because my heart was too pumped up for the words I had just heard. One by one, people walked up and put money into the offering plate. Pastor Wilson didn't take a portion for the church, nor did he want something in return. Pastor Wilson grabbed all of the bills out of the collection plate and just handed it all to me.

He then looked at me and said, "Be blessed. You don't need coins so just take the bills."

I was so filled with joy as I walked out of service, because I now had money to go buy food for at least a week. That same joy was short lived as I saw Uncle Jimmy approaching me. I was thinking to myself, "Not this dude again. He just couldn't disappear from my life?" Out of all the people that had left from my life, I was questioning why he was the one who seemed to always return. It was like an unbreakable curse. I didn't even know my uncle was there.

Uncle Jimmy walked straight up to me and snatched the money right out of my hands. He then handed me five dollars of the money and put the rest in his pocket.

Uncle Jimmy then said, "Taking care of you wasn't cheap. Well here's $5. The rest is for the living expenses when you stayed with me. Speaking of that, where are you going to stay tonight? You definitely ain't staying with me."

Talk about being lost for words. I just wanted to knock him out as my brother would say in that type of situation. I couldn't believe it. He took my money for these so-called "living expenses" and then questioned where I was going to stay? I felt like I had just been robbed. He had just snatched the money that could've covered my food expenses for about a week. He did it with ease and without second-guessing his decision. Uncle Jimmy then took off with the money in his pockets and with a big grin on his face. I tell you, this man took pride in what he did.

After basically being robbed by my uncle, I was back at square one. I needed to make money. After brainstorming ideas all day, I came up with the perfect plan to make money and get compensation for the money my uncle had just taken from me. I thought of a plan to take Uncle Jimmy's lawn mower and use it to cut grass around the neighborhood. This was during a time when kids could walk door to door in the neighborhood and offer to cut grass for a small fee. Nowadays, cutting grass is more of a business dominated by adults and landscaping companies.

With my new plan in mind, I picked a morning to go through with it. I went to my Uncle Jimmy's house in the early morning hours and took his lawnmower out of the backyard. I then pushed it about three or more miles to my adult cousin George's house that I knew needed his grass cut. My uncle and his son JJ never cut his grass, because they felt like he wouldn't pay them a fair amount. I cut the entire yard. I completed the job based on faith that he would pay me when the job was done. I didn't care about a "fair amount." At that point in my life, any amount would work for me.

I didn't really care what my uncle would say about me taking the lawnmower. I was focused on my job and making the money back that he had taken from me. While I was cutting the grass, I accidently hit a tree stump with the lawn mower and bent the blade. Luckily for me, I was already finished with cutting the yard.

George was at work, so I was hanging with his kids until he got back.

When George came back, he was so grateful for me cutting his grass and the new appearance of his lawn.

George then asked me, "How much do I owe you?"

So I said, "Whatever you can give."

It's important to know that by this time I had poison ivy. Pastor Wilson had given me some calamine lotion in the back of the church closet, which he didn't know was expired at the time. Using that expired calamine lotion caused my skin to bubble up and ooze pus.

I was expecting George to give me $10 or $15, but he gave me $40. That was more than double the money I was expecting to be paid. I couldn't believe he paid me that much money.

George even drove me to the store and bought me some poison ivy medical spray that instantaneously worked. He didn't even subtract that amount from my pay for the day. He then bought me something to eat without charging me a dime. In the end, he just had one thing to say to me.

George said, "If your uncle Jimmy asks you how much money you got paid, you say $20," and I agreed to do that if Uncle Jimmy asked me.

I always liked George. I felt like he was one of the few people who weren't scared of my uncle Jimmy. I think that's why my uncle didn't like George or want to speak to him, because George didn't fear him. My uncle Jimmy tended to only be around people he knew feared him or people he knew he could control.

I then walked back to my uncle Jimmy's house to return his lawn mower, and he was already waiting in his front yard for my return. He was beyond mad, but I didn't really care at the time. The more he hurt me, the less it hurt me. It's like I became numb to anything he did. Uncle Jimmy went on a rant about his lawnmower and then demanded that I pay an equipment fee for the lawnmower. He then asked me, "How much did he give you?"

I said, "$20," just like George had told me to say.

I then gave my uncle $10 of it, and he was like, "That's what you get for taking people's stuff. I should take all of it."

Then I let out a warm smiled and said, "You're right, Uncle."

I then walked off smiling, because I had a little more money than what he thought I had, and the lawnmower wasn't in "mint condition" anymore. To me, the joke was finally on him now. It would've been nice if that was the final joke, but it wasn't.

A couple of weeks went by and it was time for the annual family reunion. It's an event where our family members come from all over the United States to have a good time meeting other family members and bonding with them. Most of our family journeyed to town from the great state of Mississippi. During this family reunion, you're supposed to wear your best clothing. That was a problem for me. I had nothing to wear for the family reunion ex-cept for the same dirty clothes I had been wearing for months.

I started thinking of ways I could find new clothes, and I re-membered that I still had some clothes in my uncle Jimmy's house. I went back to his house, even though I wasn't allowed, and no one was there except his eldest daughter who was watching me harder than a correctional officer.

She told me, "You know you're not supposed to be here, but you can quickly get your stuff."

I managed to find a pair of my pants that my mother had got-ten me from Old Navy and a white t-shirt. I was so happy. I then took a pair of shoes and a button down shirt that JJ had in his clos-et. JJ had tons of shoes and shirts in his closet, so I figured he wouldn't miss a shirt and some old shoes, but I was completely wrong.

I made it to the family reunion, and it was a huge family turn-out. It looked like everyone was there, but my personal family was not there. No one from my grandmother's family tree line was present. My grandmother wasn't there, my mom wasn't there, my brother wasn't there, my mother's sisters weren't there, and nei-ther were their children. Even though my side of the family wasn't present, I was still surrounded by so many extended family mem-bers. I even started to slightly feel like I wasn't alone.

We had the family reunion at a local park and most of the family members were under a large tent at the park. I was under the tent laughing with some family members, and then the laughter was cut off by the sound of tires screeching in the distance. I looked over and saw my Uncle Jimmy getting out of the car. Uncle Jimmy had arrived with his son JJ, Floyd, and his older brother, Uncle Gavin. They looked beyond angry and hostile. They all exited from the car and looked directly towards me.

I was thinking to myself, "Here we go again with this dude." JJ aggressively stormed over toward me, and for the sake of my audience, I will not include the many curse words that were used by JJ.

JJ stepped up to me with his fists clinched and said, "You wearing my stuff! Take off all of my stuff right now!"

I then said, "Okay, I'll take off your stuff. Where's the bath--?"

JJ cut me off mid-sentence and said, "Nah, you gon take off my stuff right here and now! Strip down right here! You gon take off my stuff right now or you gon get beat down!"

I started to look around hoping someone would step up and stop him, but they didn't. I surveyed the crowd full of elders, adults, and children, and they all just stared at me. Just like the kids would do in school when I was bullied. Some just stared with blank expressions, and others tried to cover their faces. I was in the middle of a family reunion and everyone was completely quiet. All of my "family members" sat and watched as a 19-year-old told a 12-year-old boy to strip down in front of everyone. I was utterly in awe. It was crazy to think that JJ was talking to me this way, because he greatly feared my brother Justin. If Justin was present, JJ definitely wouldn't have been acting in the manner in which he was acting in front of everyone.

It was so quiet that you could literally hear some of the family members at the reunion scratching their heads. Once again, I felt alone. I was at an event that was full of family members, and I still felt alone. It shouldn't have been such a shock to me, considering the fact that I was also homeless in a town full of family members. I walked past family members in town on a daily basis, and I was looked down upon and seen as the "homeless kid." As far as I was concerned, this marked the day where I discovered the true definition of family, and by that definition I understood one thing—I had no family members at that reunion.

When JJ demanded that I take off everything, the adults at the reunion did as the kids did and looked out the corners of their eyes and said nothing. I gave the crowd a long stare and proceeded to take off the clothes that belonged to JJ. I gave JJ his shirt back and then took off his shoes.

Then JJ shouted, "Take it all off! Pants too!"

I then stood my own ground at that point and said, "I'm not taking off my pants."

JJ then stepped up to me with clenched fists as if he was about to hit me, and at that moment, someone took a stand. The person who took a stand had just pulled up to the family reunion, and he had already seen enough. His name is Michael or "Baby Mike."

Now let me pause and tell a little about Michael. My grandmother has three kids, all girls. Regina is the oldest, Janet is the middle child, and my mother is the youngest. Michael is my Aunt Regina's oldest son and he is just like me. He's nerdy, fun to hang around, very intelligent, and he was on his path to graduate college. Michael and JJ had extensive history together. Michael had already experienced the wrath of JJ once before when JJ beat up Michael in a barbershop, because Michael didn't show JJ the respect he felt like he deserved. JJ was a bully in the neighborhood much like his father. Michael wasn't much of a fighter and didn't want any more confrontations with JJ, but once again, they were about to cross paths.

Michael walked over to my side and stepped in front of me. Michael now stood eye to eye with JJ.

JJ then looked at Michael and said, "What you gonna do? You want to get beat up again?!"

Michael didn't back down and didn't flinch. Michael looked JJ sternly in the eye as if he wasn't afraid of him and told JJ that I wasn't taking off anything else.

Michael then turned towards me and said, "Cortez, let's get out of here. Ain't nothing but a bunch of fake family members here anyway."

We then got into his car and drove away from the reunion. I didn't understand at the time why JJ or his family just let us walk away without hurting us, but I would soon realize that they had something planned for me that night which was going to be a lot worse.

I had a lot of respect for Baby Mike. He not only came to my defense that day, but he also faced his own fears against the man who had constantly tormented and bullied him. I guess it's easier to see the light in a room full of darkness.

Michael came to my aid and said, "You're staying with us," meaning his sisters and my aunt Regina.

My aunt Regina didn't have much, but she gave all she could to me. That night, my mother had contacted my Aunt Regina and spoke with her about a plan.

My Aunt Regina told me, "Your cousin Jasmine in Texas heard how y'all have been living out there and decided to take you guys in."

Aunt Regina told me that my mother managed to purchase bus tickets for my brother and I to travel to Texas. I thought about going to Texas and thought to myself that I didn't want to be a cowboy, but I felt any place was better than where I currently lived.

Michael didn't have much gas in his car, but he managed to drive me to Madison, Illinois that night where my Aunt Janet lived. Michael dropped me off at my Aunt Janet's house, and he didn't even ask for any gas money. He just told me to be safe in Texas.

Our bus was scheduled to leave at 6am the next morning. I was happy to be in Madison, IL at my aunt's house. I was finally going to be able to see my brother again.

* * *

While I was separated from my brother, I only heard terrible stories about what was happening to him in St. Louis. I heard he was in constant fights and some guy had beat him with a pistol and threatened to kill him. I thought I was having it bad until I heard the stories about him. I cried so much after hearing that my brother was being hurt. It also broke me inside that I couldn't talk to him as much as I wanted to talk to him. When I did manage to get in contact with him, he would just tell me that everything was fine and to not worry about him. Justin never shared things like that with me. He was always strong. Justin only expressed concerned about me. I knew how protective my brother was about me, so when he would ask me how Lebanon was for me, I wouldn't tell him the truth about my uncle or me living in the streets. I would just say I was fine. I guess neither one of us wanted to worry the other.

My aunt Janet had six kids. From oldest to youngest: Katrina, Deandre, Jacoby, Ricky "Lil Ricky", Alex and Alexa. My aunt's boys all knew how to fight, were very street smart, and they were very much respected in the neighborhood. Alongside my brother, my cousins pretty much ran the neighborhood. My brother was the best male fighter in our family, and then there was Jacoby, then Ricky, then Deandre, and then me. This hierarchy is important to know for the story, because I was the baby of the group with the least amount of fighting experience and street smarts.

When Michael dropped me off at my Aunt Janet's house, no one was home except for my aunt. My cousins and my brother walked to a different neighborhood for a party. It was nighttime, and I was so exhausted from the day that I just laid on the couch thinking about the next day when I would be in Texas. I thought to myself that I could finally be far away from all of the stress I had experienced so far in my life. I would soon be in a new place with a new beginning. I just knew that life was finally going to cut me a huge break.

My hopes of a break were quickly put on hold when I heard tire screeches in the front of my aunt's house—the same sound of tire screeches that I heard at the family reunion earlier in the day. All I heard were four car doors slamming shut. I then looked over towards the door and saw my Uncle Jimmy, Uncle Gavin, JJ, and Floyd all make their way into the house in an aggressive manner.

They all came in the house to finish the dispute from the family reunion. They felt like I didn't learn my lesson that day and that I should be taught a harsher lesson. My aunt heard all of the commotion in the living room, so she walked in the room and saw them surrounding me and yelling at me. Aunt Janet quickly tried to get closer to defend me, but my uncle Gavin grabbed her and held her back.

My uncle Jimmy kept approaching saying, "You gon learn your lesson about wearing people's clothes!" JJ was mad and started walking to me with his fists clenched, but Jimmy held him back and said, "Nah, I'm gonna teach him a lesson."

Jimmy then grabbed me by the throat and slammed me against the wall. This was not a choke where he just outlined my throat and made it seem scary. He had a full grasp on my neck and lifted me from the ground while choking me against the wall. My feet were off the ground, and I couldn't breathe at all. I tried every which way to remove his grasp from my neck but nothing worked. I was a scrawny 12-year-old kid going against a 40-year-old man who had no signs of stopping. Moving his arms was like trying to push a tree over. There was nothing I could do.

My body finally gave up. My hands, which initially attempted to pry his hands off of my neck, slowly started to become weak and drop down towards the side of my body. My body had stopped fighting. I thought to myself, maybe this is how it's supposed to end. What better time to leave this earth than right now? I had nothing to live for and no life worth fighting for. I guess my brain sent that message to the rest of my body, because at that moment, my body became weaker and I started to black out. Small black dots soon became many as the oxygen was being taken away from me. My aunt's voice screaming at the top of her lungs to let me go soon became very distant, my body became motionless, and my eyes started to close.

All I wanted at that moment was to have one more hug from my mom, that's it. I would even settle to just hold her hand one more time. I just wanted a glimpse of her face to remind me of what love was. Me being choked was the new life I had come to know. Coldness, darkness, and pain replaced every bit of love that I had. This pain was a reflection of the new reality I had come to know on the streets. It felt like the end of the road for me. My world slowed down. I remember thinking, if there was a God, where was he right now?

At that very moment as I had given up life and my eyes were almost completely shut, my body dropped to the floor. I immediately started gasping for air on the ground. I was so thankful that my uncle had stopped choking me. I thought he had taken mercy on me, but he hadn't. My vision started to return to me, and as I looked up, I saw my brother with my uncle Jimmy locked in his arms and holding him high in the air. Talk about being right on time.

My brother had burst into the door, seen my uncle choking me, and he completely lost it at that point. Justin had pulled my uncle off of me, picked him up and then slammed him to the ground. My brother was 17 years old and stocky, but my uncle was 40 years old, big and fat. As Justin held my uncle in the air, I asked myself, "Where did my brother get all of this strength?" It wasn't ordinary strength. His body seemed as though it was enraged with some sort of power inside of him. My brother reminded me of Mufasa from the Lion King protecting Simba at that moment. The hyenas were my uncles, JJ and Floyd.

Justin told me his side of the story years later. He said that he and my cousins were walking to another neighborhood for a party, and then something inside had stopped him and told him to turn around and return back to the house. My cousin Ricky said it was weird, because my brother Justin stopped walking, turned around and said, "Let's go back." My brother said that he started sprinting to the house, because the voice inside of him told him to run faster back to my aunt's place. Justin said when he made it back, opened the door and saw me getting choked on the wall and gasping for air, something just took over him and he reacted.

After my brother slammed my uncle down, my other cousins stormed the house and held JJ and Floyd against the wall saying, "You tried to choke out my lil cousin bro?"

JJ and Floyd kept denying everything, but it was pretty evident what was going on in the house and what they had tried to do to me. My brother was in full rage mode, and I had never seen my uncle Jimmy so scared of a kid before in my life.

Justin finally got off of my uncle and said, "Unc, get out of my house man!"

My uncle didn't want the fight to be over and kept shouting, "Nah, nah, you wanna fight me come on! Let's fight!"

Justin just put both of his hands up and said, "Unc, just get up out the house before something happens to you man."

Uncle Jimmy then shouted back, "What's gonna happen to me huh?!"

Justin then stepped back and pulled out a pistol from his waistline. He didn't raise it up. He just held it by his side.

Uncle Jimmy's eyes got big and wide when he saw the pistol, and he shouted, "You gon shoot me?! Huh?! You gon shoot me?!"

Lil Ricky told my brother Justin to give him the gun, and Justin handed it over to Ricky.

My brother looked my uncle in his eyes and said, "You ain't worth it man."

My aunt then interrupted saying, "Y'all better calm down, because the police are outside."

The neighbors had heard all the commotion going on inside of the house, and they called the police. The police simply sat outside and watched the house. My aunt's house was well known to the police department as a location for disturbances, so they just waited outside and watched for activity.

My uncle Jimmy then stood up saying "Yeah, that's right! I'm glad the police are outside. How about I go outside and tell them that y'all mama left y'all and y'all are by y'all selves. Yeah, how about I go tell them that huh? Then y'all both gonna be split up and taken into different foster homes, and you'll never see your brother again! How about I do that?!"

My cousins tried to hold my uncle Jimmy back from going outside to tell the police, but my brother stepped up saying, "Nah, let him go," which everyone immediately did.

My brother had complete authority in that household at that moment.

Then my brother continued and said, "We ain't gonna hold you back, but I will tell you one thing. If you go outside and tell the police something and get my little brother taken away from me, I will go and get that gun. And this time, I promise you, I won't hesitate."

The stare my brother gave my uncle can't truly be described with any words. It was like two lions in the wilderness staring each other down. But in the end, my brother won that battle. My uncle's eyes became big and fearful, but my brother's eyes never twitched.

Finally, Uncle Jimmy looked at JJ, Floyd and Gavin and said, "Let's go."

Jimmy and his family then got back in their car and drove off.

After they had driven away, I stepped up to my brother and said, "I'm sorry, I didn't—" then, just like that, he cut me off.

And he said, "Go get some sleep for tomorrow."

I didn't dare question his judgment in that moment, so I went straight into the bedroom to sleep. I laid down in the bed, but I could still hear my brother in the other room yelling about what had just happened.

All I remember him saying is, "If I had been a second late, where would my brother be now? Never again man."

My brother was still outraged and didn't get a minute of sleep that night. My brother stayed up all through the night just "watching." He didn't watch for anything in particular, but it was as though he was waiting for something to happen. It was as if he had convinced himself to stay up throughout the night and not rest until his little brother was safe.

Justin woke me up the next morning at 5am and said, "Let's go."

We didn't say any goodbyes to anyone, because they were all sleep. We caught the bus to the train station, and from there we walked to the bus station and got on the charter bus.

I remember saying to my brother, "I don't want to work on a ranch in Texas, but I would like to be able to learn how to ride a horse."

My view of Texas was not very accurate at all. My brother just laughed it off and told me to try and get some sleep.

Justin woke me up as soon as we hit the city limits of Dallas, which was strange to me because I mistakenly thought that we were going to Houston at first. When I first laid eyes onto Dallas, the feeling I had in my gut was so strong. It was like love at first sight, as if Dallas was where I belonged. The feeling stayed with me that whole night. I had never felt like that before, but this place immediately evoked that feeling. I felt like the colonists when they first laid eyes on the New World—anxious with a little fear. I was afraid, not of danger, but of not being able to enjoy this moment forever. My eyes first laid sight upon a bright green neon building that I was told was the AT&T building. It marked the first sign of a new beginning and a new life for us.

When we arrived at the bus station, the bus staff very rudely threw everyone's things off of the bus. Once we got our belongings, we started to look for our ride. We made our way to the front entrance of the bus station, and my cousin, Jordan, was illegally parked in front of the building waiting for us.

He then gave us a huge Texas welcome and said, "Aye! Welcome to Texas baby!"

We all shook hands, and then we were on our way to Mesquite, Texas. I was a little relieved to not see many ranches on the drive there. My brother and my cousin Jordan who were about the same age, sat in the front of the car reminiscing about the old days in St. Louis. Jordan, his mom, and his younger siblings had once lived in the north side of St. Louis before eventually moving to Texas for a better life. We arrived at the house and greeted the rest of the family inside. I then looked outside of the window and exhaled. I thought to myself that we had successfully escaped our nightmare. I was happy to be in a new place very far from St. Louis, and for the first time in a long time, my brother and I finally got a peaceful night of rest.

CHAPTER 3:

A SHORT DREAM

We had officially moved to Mesquite, Texas to live with my cousin Jasmine. Jasmine was my great aunt Brenda's daughter, and she had three children: Jordan, Leah and Clarissa. Jordan and Leah were closer to my brother's age, and Clarissa was closer to my age. Jasmine had agreed to take my brother and I into her home, and she treated us with the best southern hospitality I had ever experienced. Living on Harvey Drive was a good time in my life. Not only did my brother and I have a new place to live, but we also had key life essentials back in our hands. We had a family, a stable home, and a good amount of food since both of her older kids worked at restaurants. Life had officially given us a fresh start and it felt nice.

My cousin Leah woke me out of my sleep on my first official morning in Texas and told me to get dressed. Leah told me that she was going to show me the neighborhood. We walked down the street to her friend's house. While she was talking with her friend in the doorway, I sat on the porch just staring off into the distance. By this time, I had the understanding that people really didn't want me around, so I tried to mind my own business and stay out of the way. I sat there staring off into the distance, until I heard her friend say something that caught my attention.

My cousin's friend said, "I think your cousin is pretty cute."

At that time, her friend's comment about me had immediately made it into my "Greatest things ever said about me" hall of fame list.

Her friend's name was Samantha, and she was a very beautiful Hispanic girl. I was very confused to why she said I was handsome, but I was also very happy at the same time. I had just left a place that completely destroyed my self-esteem and had convinced me that I was worth nothing. I was convinced at this time that no one wanted me, but here stood a girl who thought otherwise. Here was a girl who didn't talk down about me, but instead, she uplifted my spirit.

Almost every girl I had encountered in Missouri and Illinois called me ugly, but so far in Texas, I was 1 for 1. In St. Louis, I was teased by the black people and the white people, but the Hispanics in my neighborhood never teased or bullied me. In St. Louis, I wasn't exposed to the Hispanic population. I had never encountered any Hispanics before I moved to Texas, but Samantha had made my first encounter very memorable.

I remember talking to Samantha one day and telling her, "I don't know why you like me. I'm weird."

She simply responded, "Yeah, but you're the good kind of weird."

She was just trying to flood my Hall of Fame list with all of the kindness she showed me. I met many other people that day with my cousin Leah, and it felt like I was making a strong connection in the neighborhood. I wanted to accept the new faces that I was greeting, but I couldn't fully accept anyone into my life yet. I was still dealing with internal conflicts.

In public, I was one happy twelve-year-old. Things seemed to be going well in Texas, but I had an internal battle going on inside of me that I couldn't forget. My heart ached every night just thinking about my mother. My brother and I finally started making contact with her by phone, but it wasn't the same. I needed her there with me. I felt very distant from my mom. We would never go past the surface level of a conversation. Every time I asked her about her life, she would quickly change the subject. It was like she was avoiding any question about her or her current state in life. After awhile, I just stopped asking questions altogether. I only knew that she had moved to New Jersey but that was the furthest she would elaborate.

I would often hear my cousin Jasmine arguing with my mom on the phone saying, "Your son is over here crying for you every night!"

I literally cried myself to sleep every night. My eyes would eventually get sore and dry out, and I'd go to bed afterwards. My mind was constantly fighting questions throughout the night. I would ask myself "Did she really love me? How could she do this? Is she ever coming back?" In the midst of my everlasting thoughts, I would also hear my uncle's voice yelling at me to "face reality" and "no one wants you." My uncle's voice haunted my dreams almost every night. Even now, I can hear his voice as clear as day.

One night I told myself that I wasn't going to cry anymore. I had accepted that the worse was behind me, and I felt that my new life was about to begin without trouble this time. I knew that if I kept crying, my mother would be yelled at more by my cousin Jasmine, and I didn't want my mother being in trouble because of me. Even though my mom had left and I was hurt, my love for her never left. I was mad at her, but I couldn't cause harm onto my mom. I was sad and heartbroken that she wasn't by my side, but I never held any hate towards my mom. I've never been that type of person. In all honesty, I was just happy to have a little communication with her. My mother being absent from my life wasn't the only thing that was upsetting me.

I was also really upset about school. I know that most kids would be ecstatic to not go to school again, but not me. I was a weird kid and one huge nerd. School was all I ever knew. I actually enjoyed learning things. We tried almost everyday to enroll me in school, but Texas had one tough system. It felt nearly impossible to enroll in school. Everything required my mother to be present to physically sign enrollment papers or to sign over temporary custody. I had very limited contact with my mother, and she did not have any plans on flying down to Texas to enroll me in school.

Time went by, and the urge to go to school grew tremendously. Academics were very important to me. I would show my younger cousin Clarissa old math problems and English assignments so that I could retain the information I was taught previously in school.

My cousins would always say, "You are extremely smart."

And I would just think in my head, "Yeah, but for how long?" I knew that the material I was taught in school would eventually start to fade away from my head and that thought by itself caused me to worry and panic about my academic future. I kept hoping that my mom would one day come to Texas and enroll me in school and everything would be fine. It was only a matter of time. Things were going to change for the better, and I had to keep hope alive. At least I thought things were going to change.

One morning, my cousin Jasmine informed us that she was moving back to St. Louis, because she missed her family. Upon hearing these words, I felt like my heart dropped. I couldn't believe what she had just told us and what was about to happen. It felt like a nightmare. After staying with my cousin Jasmine for only a few months, we now had to move on. She was basically saying that we needed to find another place to live, because she would be moving back soon.

My brother contacted our mom, and she said that she would see what she could do about finding us a new place to live.

After waiting around for about a week, my mother contacted us and said, "I found you guys a place to stay. You're going to be moving back to St. Louis with your Aunt Janet."

Talk about a showstopper. Here I was having the time of my life in Texas and now I was being told that I'd be returning to the very place that tore me apart. I'd be returning to the very house where I was nearly choked to death and the same streets my brother had almost been shot in. Here we were being told that we'd have to relive the very nightmare we had moved to Texas to escape. Even though I dreaded the thought of going back, I had no way to change the decision. My mother had already booked the bus tickets, and my Aunt Janet had already been informed of our arrival time.

My Aunt Janet and cousins weren't that bad, but the neighborhood and everything around them proved otherwise. I sat on the bus ride to St. Louis thinking about all the horrors that awaited us. With every positive thought I tried to picture in my mind, another dark thought came and destroyed it. I continued my web of thoughts until we finally arrived at my aunt Janet's house.

The first feelings I had walking into that house were awful. I just kept staring at the very wall that I was choked on. It kept sending chills throughout my body. I kept getting chills in my head thinking about the incident with my uncle Jimmy. When I looked at the wall, I got flashbacks of the incident and my breathing felt like it was constricted. It was PTSD at its finest. There wasn't much I could do to fight the feeling away, so I told myself that I had to learn how to live with it. I didn't want to be in that house, but I didn't have any other choice. My brother Justin wasn't as thrilled to be back in town either, but he quickly got over it.

My Aunt Janet already had six kids of her own (Katrina, Deandre, Jacoby, Ricky "Lil Ricky", Alex and Alexa), but she agreed to welcome in two more. Due to so many kids being in the house, we all slept on pallets as alternatives to beds. Pallets are a combination of blankets laid out on the floor for a big group of people to sleep on. You were lucky if you got a pillow. My cousins never really had much, so basic essentials were always in short supply. My mother had sent a care package to my aunt's house the first week I was there. The package was filled with food and some other items. After about a week, it was all gone. My cousins would take things out of the package on a daily basis until it all vanished. Eight kids in one house in the hood was not a good combination for success.

We lived with my aunt many times in the past since we were always bouncing around homes, but this time just felt different. It felt as though I was trapped in this neighborhood forever. Even though the negative thoughts were in full force in my head, living with my aunt wasn't all bad. Some of the negatives actually made me a stronger person.

Living with my aunt taught me one key aspect in life. It taught me how to survive. When you have ten people living in one house with no jobs, you had to find ways to make money and survive. Government assistance was very limited, and it didn't provide much help for our household. I'll just leave it at that. We all had a curfew in my aunt's home. If you weren't back in the house at a certain hour, then you were locked outside. So, we ran the streets all day and returned back in the late evening time just before the doors were locked for the night. My cousins made their living by engaging in different "assortments of activities that would not hold a very high moral rating amongst individuals secluded from that particular neighborhood." In short, they did what they had to do. That's all I'll say about their lifestyles and occupations.

I wasn't as experienced at "street survival" like my cousins. My cousins had been living in rough neighborhoods their entire lives and learned ways to survive and make money. I was just a young, nerdy, punk kid who had a roaring stomach. I had learned some survival skills while I was homeless in Lebanon, but my aunt's neighborhood was a different beast. Lebanon was a small town and didn't have much activity, but this neighborhood was filled with gangs, drugs, and constant "put your life in danger" activity. Because of this, I quickly picked up street skills from my cousins.

My family in one word were "hustlers." They taught me how to be a hustler too. Hustlers are basically "go getters" who make ends meet no matter what and don't quit. They taught me skills that would be useful for my childhood and adulthood life.

Besides poverty in itself, the environment made it even harder to survive. It was full of crime like robberies, burglaries, and drug dealing. I saw drugs constantly pushed through the neighborhood and dope fiends, people who are addicted to drugs, wander the streets all day and night. Often times they were homeless and wandered the streets or live in abandoned houses. After a few months of living with my aunt, I could tell a drugged-out person (crackhead, dope fiend, clucker, bum, etc.) from a mile away, and I could tell who was moving dope.

It was very common for people from our neighborhood to go to a more prosperous neighborhood to rob them. The robbers from our neighborhood thought that the families in prosperous neighborhoods had plenty to give, but it was up to the robbers to help those families distribute the wealth. It was sort of like a Robin Hood mentality, except for the fact that these guys in the neighborhood robbed both the rich and the poor. They robbed with equality.

Drugs were everywhere and trouble was behind every corner. I had to make a living if I wanted to survive in this neighborhood, so I did what I was taught—I hustled. I did almost every small job

I could think of that would earn me cash but also keep me out of handcuffs. I ran to the store for people and they would let me keep the change, I picked up food for people and cleaned rooms. I did whatever small job I could find so that I could eat at the end of the day. The money wasn't great, but it was better than nothing.

At the end of most of my small jobs, I was given one dollar for a job well done. I would then take that dollar and run to the store. At the store, they used to sell 25-cent cakes (now they're like 50 cents each), and I would buy four of them. We called them "quarter cakes" at the time. I had developed a mind trick that consisted of quantity and not quality. I told myself that if I ate something for the day, I would be fine. It didn't matter if it was a snack or real food. I just needed to eat something to survive for the day. I felt as long as I kept buying 4 quarter cakes each day, I would be fine. Sometimes I got lucky and earned enough to be able to buy a honeybun that cost 35 cents. Buying a honeybun was only on special occasions when I got a "work bonus." It wasn't too often that I was able to buy it, but I was happy on the days that I could.

I learned new mannerisms on the streets. I learned how to live, how to talk, walk, conduct yourself, talk to women (which I failed at), and how to survive. I tried hustling as much as I could, but it was an endless task. Times got harder and business became bad for me. People stopped sending me to the store and all of my other side jobs vanished. I was back on the streets searching for food again. After failing to find food outside of the house, I decided to sneak some food out of my aunt's room.

My aunt quickly found out that food was missing from her room, and she went on a complete rampage throughout the house searching for the person who took it. I started envisioning the painful butt whooping she was going to give me when she found out that it was me. My brother saw the guilty look on my face, and he immediately stepped up and told my aunt that he was the one that took the food from her room. Even when I was wrong, my brother always had my back and took the rap for me. He always protected me. My brother and aunt got into a huge argument that day, which resulted in my brother being kicked out of the house. He went back to running from house to house in St. Louis. Justin ("J-Rock") was not a man of many words. He simply gathered his belongings and left the house.

Justin's protection was nothing new to me. He even protected me when he wasn't around. One day I walked to the basketball court down the street from my house. I asked the guys playing on the court, "Hey, do you mind if I play?"

And they went from 0 to 100. I had forgotten about the golden rule of "Don't talk to people you don't know." Breaking this rule was an immediate initiation for a fight. They got so mad and started running over to me so that they could beat me up. Yeah, it was that serious. One of the guys in the group was the boldest and decided he'd step up and take the first swing at me. He started approaching me with his fist clenched, and I started back-peddling towards my escape route.

Just when the guy was within a couple feet of me charging up his punch, one of the other guys stopped him and yelled, "Ay man stop! You better chill out! You know who that is?!"

I was waiting for the next words thinking to myself, "Who am I?"

He then continued, "That's J-Rock's brother!"

After that was said, the guy in front of me developed a very sickly look across his face and his eyes got very big.

He immediately grabbed the basketball and tossed it in front of me saying, "Oh snap, my bad bro! Here go the ball. Ay, tell J-Rock I meant no disrespect. I don't want any problems with him. I'm sorry bro. I ain't know you was his lil bro."

I grew tough after hearing that and snatched the ball up from him like, "Yeah, there's going to be some changes around here!"

Just kidding, but I should've said that. I just simply took the ball and shot around the basketball court for awhile. The guy even let me keep the ball. He was such a nice guy after learning that I was J-Rock's little brother.

Later on, I told my brother what had occurred that day, and he demanded to know the name of the guy who tried to hit me. I kept telling him that the guy apologized, but my brother and my cousins went down to the court themselves, found the guy, and had a very "friendly conversation" with him. This was something my brother and cousins did really well. They protected and looked out for one another, especially the three youngest in the house, which included me. My brother's one pet peeve that he took to heart was "don't mess with my little brother." He lived by that rule.

* * *

After my brother was kicked out of my Aunt Janet's house and my sources of income were cut off in the neighborhood, I encountered a horrible challenge in my life—starvation. My stomach was so hungry and my body was very weak. I was already a really scrawny kid and not eating made it even worse. At that point of hunger, my body was prepared to eat anything regardless of the consequences.

I opened the refrigerator, not caring if the food belonged to my aunt, but the fridge was completely empty. There weren't even any snacks in her room. I couldn't find anything to eat after demolishing all of the bread and syrup the house had to offer earlier in the week. I looked on the side door inside of the fridge and saw a bottle of children's cold medicine. My brain saw the medicine as food. I remember grabbing the bottle and thinking to myself if this was the right thing to do. I guess the thought process wasn't under much review in my head, because within a couple of seconds I had opened the bottle. I had told myself that I would only drink a little, but my body was so weak and hungry. As soon as I tasted the medicine, I started chugging it down. I was so hungry. The only thing that kept my body from drinking the whole thing was telling myself that I had to save some for later. Out of desperation and survival, the medicine was food for me. My body took what it could and told my mind that we weren't going to starve to death today. My body was locked in survival mode.

Living in the hood was just about survival. Each and everyday was about survival. Not school, not a job, not love, but survival. The neighborhood above anything else made me tough. It taught me not to be fearful. I saw danger every night. I saw things that I'm not even allowed to speak of anywhere at any point in time. I was a naturally quiet person, but the neighborhood taught me how to keep my mouth shut and my head down. These were all keys to survival in the neighborhood.

There were about 20 guys posted on the block (the street) every single night. I remember staring at them and saying to myself, "Is that all life is in this neighborhood? Standing there doing the same thing everyday? Worrying about survival on a daily basis? Going nowhere? Is that my future? No, it can't be. No, it won't be." I had made a choice, and that choice was to never be one those guys. I had to be different and make better decisions than they did.

I used everything I was learning on the streets, and I created a system that best worked for me. I wanted to survive in the neighborhood, but I didn't want to change who I truly was inside. I wanted to be the best version of myself with the skills I had acquired from the street. I tried to change in the past, but nothing ever felt right. I never felt like "me." I knew that just being me was the best option for my life.

Living in my aunt's dangerous neighborhood caused me to have more exposure to the local police department. Even though a few of their officers caused trouble in the neighborhood, I was happy to see a police patrol car passing by. I felt like nothing could touch me when their cars passed by me on the streets. I had never been on the wrong side of the law before, so I was always calm when I saw them.

One day, I woke up to walk my little cousin Alex to school. I walked him to school almost every day since it was a rough neighborhood and he was only in elementary school. When we stepped outside of the house, a police squad car was sitting directly in front of the house. I was naturally calm since I didn't do anything wrong. Two officers got out of the car and started walking towards me.

One of the officers looked at my cousin Alex and said, "You might as well start walking to school by yourself buddy because your brother's gonna be with us for awhile."

I told my cousin to hurry and walk to school, and I turned back towards the officers and asked "Is there something wrong?"

The officers responded by saying, "We'll ask the questions. Who else is in that house with you?"

I quickly responded, "No one. Just me."

The officers informed me that they were looking for my cousins, and I told him that I had no idea where they were at right now. At the time, it was neighborhood law not to give officers information, especially not to these two officers who were in front of me. Both of them were well known in the neighborhood as two cops who didn't "play by the rules." As I'm speaking to the officers, my cousin Deandre walked out of the house.

The officer looked at me and said, "No one's here huh?"

I quickly tried to play it off by saying, "Did you get home late last night?"

The officer didn't buy any of it and handcuffed both of us. I had never seen this side of the police before in my life since I had never been to jail before. I was now getting a first-hand look at the full arrest procedure. They slammed my cousin's head on the hood of the car and threw me into the back of the squad car. They took us to the police station and gave me a mug shot photo. The cop told me that he was very surprised that I wasn't already in the criminal system on his computer.

He asked me, while pointing to the computer screen, "Is this you?"

It was some random black guy who looked nothing like me and had the name "Brian Johnson."

I simply responded, "No."

After the police officers finished asking me questions in the interrogation room, they brought me outside where my aunt's boyfriend was waiting to pick me up. The police officers told him that I got arrested for not being in school at that time of day. I knew that was false, because I got arrested around 7:30am for not being in a school that started at 8:30am. Something didn't add up there. I knew they just wanted my cousins, and every bit of information they could possibly get about them.

That wasn't my last bad run in with those two officers. The next incident happened shortly after the first. My aunt's boyfriend, Clarence, had hit her. My cousin Deandre went to defend his mom, but he got the worse of Clarence's wrath. Clarence picked up my cousin and through him through the wall in the house. My cousin stormed out of the door, and no one knew where he went. I was worried about him and feared that maybe her boyfriend would turn to me next. My brother was gone at the time, along with both of my older boy cousins, Lil Ricky and Jacoby, who had left with him.

In a matter of about fifteen minutes, I heard a knock at the door saying, "This is the police, open up!"

When they knocked on the door, I was at an equal distance from the door as I was from my aunt. Both my aunt and the police officer were yelling orders at me.

The blinds to the window were open, and the police officer looked through the window and yelled, "Come open this door right now!"

I then looked towards my aunt who told me, "Don't open that door!"

I looked back at the officer and he repeated "Open this door right now!"

I looked back towards my aunt who once again told me, "You better not open that door!"

My head felt like it was spinning from the mixed orders I was receiving from both sides. My body was frozen solid. I finally made my decision to listen to my aunt because I didn't have to live with that police officer.

Meanwhile, Clarence had managed to get on top of the roof and jump over to the neighbor's yard without being seen. The officer at the front door then rammed the door open and made his way inside.

When the officer came inside of the house, he came straight towards me, pushed me down to the ground and said, "Next time I tell you to open this door, you better do what the heck I say!"

I'm censoring the officer's words, but he was yelling multiple curse words at me. Then another officer came from the backdoor and both of them demanded to see my aunt's boyfriend.

The officer at the front door said, "Where is he? I know he's here. He probably ran. I went to school with him, I know he'd run."

The officers then turned their attention towards my aunt and directed everyone in the house to line up on the wall.

The officer started yelling at my aunt saying, "You like guys who beat on you and your kids? You like guys who throw kids through walls? You sure do know how to pick them. What if I threw one of your kids through the wall right now?"

He started to scan the room and eventually locked eyes with me. My heart started pounding, and my anxiety was raised to a new height that day. I will never forget his name. Officer Burt. Officer Burt was a heavy set white guy with a buzzed haircut and a flustered red face. He became the sole reason I didn't like police officers.

Officer Burt approached me and said, "Yeah, what if I pushed him through the wall right now?"

He then proceeded to push me twice into the wall before slapping me across the head.

I started crying and my aunt said, "If you touch my nephew again, I promise you won't have a job tomorrow."

These weren't officers—these were bullies. I never liked bullies.

Then Officer Burt let out a smirk and said, "Let's get out of here. This place stinks anyway. All these freaking kids in this house, it's like the Cosby show in here. Next time I come back here, you better have this place cleaned up."

My aunt had a witty response for every witty comment stated by the officers, but I was more focused on Officer Burt. That's who my eyes were locked on, and that's who I always remembered. I vowed I would never forget his name. A bully with a badge. I couldn't believe officers could do something like that and get away with it. At that moment, Officer Burt had caused me to lose faith in police officers. I felt like I couldn't trust any of them anymore.

After the officers left, my cousin Deandre finally returned back to the house, and my aunt gave him a mouthful about calling the police.

She yelled at him, "What's wrong with you? Those officers just came in and beat up on Tez. Now he's crying because of you."

My cousin just shook his head and said, "I just wanted them to come and scare your boyfriend off. I just wanted that dude gone. I didn't mean for them to hurt Tez." Deandre started crying and said, "I couldn't sit back here and watch you get hit ma." Deandre then looked towards me and said, "I'm sorry Tez man. I didn't mean for anything to happen to you."

While Deandre was talking to me, my brother had made his way back into the house along with my other cousins Lil Ricky and Jacoby.

My brother asked, "Why is Tez crying?"

My cousin Deandre briefed him on everything that happened, and my brother's eyes flared up. I had to thank God that my brother wasn't there when Officer Burt was pushing me around, or my brother would've been in prison that night for assault on two police officers.

My aunt's boyfriend Clarence came busting through the back door angry beyond reasonable explanation. Clarence didn't want the fight to be over between him and my cousin Deandre. He wanted to give payback to my cousin for calling the cops on him and almost going to jail.

Clarence clenched his fist and started making his way towards my cousin saying, "You gon call the police on me huh?! You called the police?!"

My cousin took one step back away from him. It was obvious that my cousin Deandre didn't want to fight my aunt's boyfriend. My cousin was only a teenager and my aunt's boyfriend was a grown man who had been in and out of prison.

My aunt's boyfriend started charging his fist up to punch my cousin, but he was stopped dead in his tracks by a hand—my brother's hand. Justin had stopped Clarence in his tracks. I don't think anyone reading this book truly understands how big of a moment this was unless you lived in that house. Clarence was known as one of the toughest guys in the neighborhood. Clarence was at the top of the food chain in the household and no one ever challenged his ruling in the house. But at that moment, my brother had no regard as to what the hierarchy was in that house or the neighborhood. Justin always said that he was never much into resumes of other people. Justin decided to take a stand.

Justin started listing off the wrongs that Clarence had committed throughout the day. Justin stared at Clarence with the same menacing eyes he gave my uncle Jimmy when he confronted him in the past.

Justin stared at him and told him, "You beat my aunt, threw my cousin through the wall, and caused my little brother to get hurt and cry!"

It was as though my brother had already labeled my aunt's boyfriend Clarence as guilty. Justin was now on the offense, but Clarence took his challenge.

Clarence stepped up to my brother and said, "What the heck did you just say to me lil punk?! Janet, you better get yo nephew before I knock him out too!"

I was sure my brother would step down, but he didn't move a step. I would've been terrified in his position to be going against someone who was extremely feared, but my brother Justin wasn't scared.

Clarence attempted to take a step forward towards my cousin, and Justin once again held his hand up and blocked him. I was very afraid for my brother. I knew he was running out of chances to back down from the fight, and I didn't want to see him get hurt. But my brother, as always, didn't care.

Justin said, "You need to get up out my house!"

Clarence quickly responded with a laugh and said, "Yo house?? Punk, I paid for this house. Man you better...you know what...let me leave before I knock you out."

His constant repetition of the phrase "knock you out" surely evoked some emotions from my brother, since he was using my brother's favorite phrase.

My brother's stance was locked in and strong. He had done the unthinkable and stood face to face against the menace himself. There was a brief sigh of relief in the house, because Clarence had just stated that he was going to leave. We probably should've waited a couple more seconds before exhaling on that thought, because Clarence completed a slight turn as if he was going to leave but then tried to turn around and throw a quick cheap shot at my brother. My brother saw his punch coming from a mile away and dodged it and grabbed Clarence. My brother had so much power and control of the fight that my aunt Janet had to try and pull my brother off of him, but my brother had one more idea. Clarence was trying so desperately to get away from the machine known as my brother, but it wasn't happening anytime soon. Justin picked up Clarence by the collar, and slung him through the wall. Clarence landed right next to the same hole he made when he threw my cousin Deandre through it. Either we needed some stronger walls in the house or my brother possessed sheer power that seemed to amaze us every day.

Justin told Clarence once again, "Get out of my house!"

This time, Clarence didn't hesitate to leave or try to throw a cheap shot. All of his toughness had been replaced by fear and he quickly grabbed his jacket and left through the door. My brother was now the one at the top of the chain in that house, and no one dared to question it. We all just sat there in amazement at what had just taken place. A kid had taken a grown man's role.

I asked my brother Justin years later where that kind of power had come from and he said, "I don't know. Once Deandre told me what happened I just knew I had to do something. I wasn't just gonna sit back and watch it happen again. No one messes with my brother or my family. If I ever see that dude again, boy I'd knock him right in his face."

My brother Justin told me to never do what he does or live like he lives. He taught me to always fight for what I feel is right, but never fight just to prove you're tougher or to impress anyone. Only fight when you have to fight. Once again, I adopted his values and made them my law. My brother told me that respect would get me much further than fear would ever get me. He said that bullies eventually get what's coming to them. I wholeheartedly respected my brother. My brother Justin was now the protector of the entire household.

All of my cousins greatly respected my brother too.

I once asked my cousin Deandre, "Why did you drop out of school?"

My cousin looked at me and said, "Once your brother Justin left East Side High School, I said heck no! I'm outta here! Your brother always protected more people than just you. Once he left, a whole group left right behind him."

East Side was a school that you had to have protection to attend. My brother had been that protector for a lot of kids and that's why they respected him. They could go to school and learn without having fear of getting beat up because my brother J-Rock was there to protect them. No matter who talked about him, they always said the same thing—"I have nothing but respect for J-Rock." Once I heard that, I didn't want to be like anyone else. I wanted to be like my brother.

We had just witnessed the unthinkable. My cousins and I had watched my brother beat up my aunt's boyfriend and forced him to leave the house. Justin stayed up all night, sitting on the couch just waiting for her boyfriend to come back, but he didn't come back. Clarence refused to come back as long as my brother was there. Justin was our protector.

I had contacted my mom afterwards and briefed her about everything that had just happened. My mother agreed that we needed to get out of that neighborhood because it was highly dangerous for us. Justin then took the phone from me and gave my mom a full speech on our conditions and what we had been enduring throughout our stay at my aunt's house. My mother agreed to send us money for food and a Greyhound bus ticket to anywhere we wanted to live. Living with her wasn't an option.

Justin came to me afterwards and asked, "Where do you want to go? You choose."

I looked back at him and gave a big "family reunion" smile. Without much thought, I looked at him and said, "Texas!"

My brother and I managed to purchase two one-way bus tickets to Dallas that would depart in just a few days. When the day finally came, Lil Ricky and Deandre escorted us to the Greyhound Bus Station. Justin wasn't overly ecstatic about leaving my cousins there to defend the house against the wrath of my aunt's boyfriend.

My cousin Deandre looked at my brother and said, "J-Rock we cool man. This is our life bro. We been living like this. You better get on that bus before I take yo ticket and go myself."

I was sad that I had a way out, and my cousins who protected me against bullies, drug dealers, and even cops would now be stuck in the place of utter destruction. I missed my cousins a lot when we eventually departed from the city.

My favorite cousin was Ricky, and before we got on the bus, I had a long conversation with him. I told Ricky about what my uncle Jimmy had said to me in the church parking lot about no one wanting me. I told him that it greatly affected my self-esteem and made me feel worthless.

Ricky looked at me and told me, "People like that want to bring you down because they ain't nothing themselves. Don't listen to people like that. You smart man. You ain't out here in the streets like us. You got a chance to be better than all of us. Do work in Texas. We gon need someone to look up to out here. We know you gon be somebody. Just don't forget us man. Know we always here to watch after you, and if I need to go to Texas to beat some people up, I will!"

Ricky always had my back a lot like my brother.

My brother and I finally got on our bus to Dallas and took off, leaving everything behind in the distance. I closed my eyes and said to myself, "I'm never coming back to this place," and I meant it. We arrived in Texas about 16 hours later, but the same dream we had experienced before was long gone and a tougher reality had taken its place. We arrived in Texas with new challenges waiting for us. The roller-coaster ride in my life was very far from over, but Texas had something special in store for us.

CHAPTER 4:

FINDING CHANGE

W e had officially made our way back to Dallas, Texas, and I couldn't have been more excited. As I mentioned before, things were not the same as when we first came to Texas. This time we moved in with our cousin Jordan. Jordan was the person who had picked us up from the bus station the first time we came to Dallas, Texas. Jordan was staying in an apartment complex with two other familiar people from earlier in the story—Cora and Nora. They were all my brother's age and older, so I was the young one in the group. We all stayed in a one-bedroom apartment together in north Dallas. Since my brother and I were the newcomers who didn't have a dollar to our names, we got the luxury of sleeping in the living room. This really wasn't a problem for us considering the living conditions we had just moved from in St. Louis.

It was a very poor apartment complex, but it was livable. That's all that mattered to us. Glamour wasn't a key thing for us anymore. It was all about having the basic essentials in life. Food, water, clothing, and shelter were the only things we really needed to survive. We even went without electricity from time to time. We did whatever it took to survive. Everyone in the house chipped in money for food and made sure everyone ate. The chemistry between everyone in the house seemed to be growing over time. We didn't all know each other that well at first, but we quickly became family and developed love and trust for one another. Good company can make any neighborhood seem livable.

Then in the midst of everything, something magical happened—I turned thirteen. I couldn't believe that I had finally turned a year older. It felt like I had been twelve for about twenty years already. There wasn't much of a celebration or even a party, but I was thankful that I made it past a year that felt like a curse for me. Instead of dwelling on the past year, I decided to focus on the present with my newfound family.

Everything seemed to be going well until one day we received a note from the apartment leasing office telling us that we had less than a month to move out. The entire apartment complex had been bought out by a big company and everyone who stayed there had to find a new place to live. Once again, we were on the move.

We never stayed in a single place for too long. By this time, my brother and I were experts at packing our stuff and moving to another place. We understood that each place we moved to was only temporary. Sooner or later we would have to move. This time around, we spent many hours each day searching for a new place to live and finally found a new apartment. I was so happy that the hunt for a place to live was finally over. The only apartment we could afford as a group was a small studio apartment with six people to share it. Nora's boyfriend Theo had left his parents house and decided to move with us as well. The apartment was very cramped, but it was all that we could afford.

Aside from the cramped apartment, I still had a huge problem—school. We literally tried every single day to enroll me in school, but Forest Meadow Middle School wouldn't take me unless my mom personally came to enroll. I was so upset. I would walk miles up to Forest Meadow MS just to ask a single question so that I could get a peek at school life again. I even walked to Forest Meadow towards the end of the school day so I could make it in time for the last bell and walk home with the rest of the kids just to feel like I was a part of it.

Cora knew that I was hanging around Forest Meadow and she, along with her sister Nora, marched up to the school and demanded every which way to get me in school, but nothing ever worked. We even tried Lake Highlands Middle School, but they gave us the same response as Forest Meadow. Desperate times led to finding a woman to pretend to be my mom, but the school still didn't buy it.

One administrator told me "Wow, you are definitely one of the more passionate kids about learning, and if there was something I could do I would, but we need your actual mother here to handle this paperwork."

It was a devastating feeling to have the compassion for school but not have the means to get in. While school continued to make it more difficult for me to return, I still had other areas of my life that caused me to worry.

Problems became worse in the household. Rent was short in coming, and the rest of the house occupants demanded the monthly installment of rent from my brother and I. We called our mom for help, but she said that she wouldn't be able to help us. This led to a huge argument between my brother Justin and my cousin Jordan about rent money. As a result, Justin told them we didn't have our half of the rent. Justin was a man of much pride and said that we weren't staying somewhere that we weren't welcome. He told me to grab my stuff, and we started walking down the road.

Justin took us to his girlfriend's house, but she said that we couldn't stay with her and told us to immediately get out of her house. We had no place to live and no other direction to go. Thank God we received a call from my grandmother's sister, Aunt Paula, who just so happened to live in Dallas. She took us into her home for the night, and found us an apartment in Garland, Texas. It was just a studio apartment, but at least it was just us this time.

Living in Garland was tough. Justin couldn't find a job, and food was by far the hardest thing to come by in the house. We didn't have much to eat at all, and there were times when we didn't eat for days. Each day I would walk up and down the street looking for coins that were dropped on the ground. If I found a dime I was a very lucky man, because it saved me the time of having to find ten pennies. A quarter was very rare to find, but if it was found, that meant luck was in my favor for the week. I mostly found dirty pennies. That was my job. I was that dirty kid walking up and down the street kicking leaves and rocks around hoping to find the slightest bit of change on the ground.

One day when I was walking down the street, I found a quarter on the ground. I almost cried at the sight of it. I felt as though I had won a million bucks. I quickly picked up the quarter and added it to my week's total, which came out to an even fifty cents. I took it and ran directly to the store. My stomach hadn't tasted any food in almost a week, and I was sure I was on the road of starvation. My stomach constantly growled and my head was always light.

When I made it to the store, I quickly grabbed 2 quarter cakes and slammed the 50 cents onto the store counter. The store worker then calculated the total with tax, which was more than what I had. I had completely forgotten about tax. I told him that I didn't have more than the 50 cents on the counter, and the store worker allowed me to purchase the two cakes without paying tax. I was so happy to finally have something to eat, and I sat outside of the store and devoured the first cake in a matter of seconds. I started to open the second cake I had bought, but then I stopped. I couldn't eat it. I put it in my pocket and then started running back to the house.

My brother was lying down asleep in the bed. My brother always gave me food when he had it and always made sure I ate first. I knew that his time without food was probably a lot longer than mine. I sat the quarter cake down next to my brother and went back outside to continue my search for change.

When it started becoming dark outside, I decided to call it a night. I returned back to the house, and when I made it back inside, my brother was sitting up and his eyes were red and watery. The cake was gone and only the wrapper remained.

My brother leaned over to me and said, "Thank you. You're a good brother."

That's all it took—a simple quarter cake to show love to my brother. I gave my brother a hug and we both started crying together. I had never seen my brother cry before so it made me even sadder to see his tears. I didn't fear death nor starvation, but I feared losing my brother most of all. Seeing him in pain always broke my heart.

My brother later admitted to me that he was totally surprised and happy to see the cake laying next to him, because it showed him that he wasn't in this alone. I had his back and he had mine. That's all we really needed. My brother was also sad that we had to resort to picking off scraps and searching for dirty coins on the ground to make a living. He said this wasn't how we were supposed to live. That put me at ease to know at a time of our lowest, my brother still had high hopes of making things happen for us. A 19-year-old kid taking care of a 13-year-old kid, talking about surviving together. He told me not to ever accept defeat that easily in my life. We might have been hit hard by poverty, but it did nothing but increase our hunger to get out of that situation.

God provided us with a way out when my cousin Jordan called us the next day and said, "Hey, we just moved. Y'all still need a place to stay?"

We quickly took Jordan up on his offer and moved to North Dallas with him. We moved into an apartment complex positioned right on Shady Brook Lane. I had almost abandoned hope in this world, but hope was restored in me. If I knew God's plan at the time, then I probably would've realized that the move to the Shady Brook Apartments was going to be a huge turning point in my life. I didn't see God's plan at the time, but he definitely had one for me. I personally saw no point in moving from Garland back to North Dallas, but great things were awaiting me in Dallas. All we had to do was pack our things and move there—which we did.

CHAPTER 5:

BACK INTO THE GAME

My brother and I were now living with my cousin Jordan, Nora, Cora, and Theo in North Dallas. Another summer passed and another school year was approaching. With the faith I still had remaining, I tried one last time to call my mother and convince her to come to Texas and enroll me in school. I seriously didn't think she was going to come because two years had passed, and she still hadn't come to do it. The world was moving on without me, and I was starting to believe that I would never be back in school again. Then something changed. I received a phone call from my mother saying that she had booked a flight to Texas and she was coming to enroll me in school. I was so happy to hear that, but I was also a little skeptical. This wasn't the first time I had heard these words from her, so I wasn't sure how much I could really trust them.

I didn't completely buy into the dream of my mom coming to Texas and enrolling me into school, but I had a little hope inside of me. Hope turned to reality the moment we pulled up to the airport and saw my mom waiting with her luggage in front of the airport arrival doors. My mom looked the same as when I had last seen her.

She stood in front of the airport looking lost as ever. I couldn't believe it. It was real, but it felt like a dream. It had more than two years since I last laid eyes upon my mother, and here she was standing in front of me. Here stood the woman that I would cry myself to sleep thinking about, and the same woman I had dreamed of hugging one more time when my uncle had my life in his hands. I was really staring at her.

All of the negative emotions I had towards her for leaving us were nowhere in sight, nor did I question her about anything in the past. All I remember was running full speed at her and hugging her so tight that she couldn't even lift her own arms to hug back. My mother held more power in my life than just being my mom who had left. She also held the key to my education and my only hope of getting back into the school life I had missed so much. I was not only hugging my mother, but my missing life as well.

My brother then approached my mom, and for the second time in my life, I watched my brother cry. It was truly a moment that I'll never forget. Everything that my heart could ask for on this earth was embedded into one woman. I could feel God's presence at that moment. Love was definitely in the air, and hate/anger was long gone. That moment was so surreal. There was no place for harsh words or judgment. It was a moment that was only meant to be cherished.

After welcoming my mom into Texas, we made our way back to our apartment. When my mother first entered the house, she was welcomed with warm smiles and greetings from everyone. Everyone started crying, because the look on my face had life again. Being out on the streets, having to grow up quickly, missing out on childhood, and just moving from place to place every other week had taken its toll on me and my physical appearance. My face was more stern, my eyes were more cold and the words I spoke echoed the life of a matured man.

I don't remember saying much of anything to my mom. I just wanted to enjoy the moment with her. When my mom came to Texas, that lost boy inside of me was brought back to life. Everyone in the house had seen that look on my face and could do nothing else but smile and cry. Everyone was excited for her return, but I wanted to make sure that we made the most out of her time in Texas.

The very first task we pursued was getting me back into school. I had already been waiting two years for this to happen. My nerves were on edge because I wanted everything to flow smoothly in the enrollment process. It was not simple. My mother was not a resident of Texas, so we had to fight a lot of legal and technical battles throughout the day before I could even step foot into a Texas school. After handling everything to establish legal residency, we finally made our way over to Sam Tasby Middle School. I was so excited at how close I was to enrolling into school.

We were finally at the last stage in the enrollment process at Sam Tasby when I heard one of the ladies behind the desk say, "Uh oh, wait."

I thought she was about to tell me that I wouldn't be able to enroll in school.

The woman continued saying, "You're not in our school's jurisdiction. It says here that you'll actually be enrolling in Benjamin Franklin Middle School and not Sam Tasby Middle School."

The office staff advised my mother and I that they would forward the enrollment papers to Benjamin Franklin Middle School. I was a little disappointed, but I cared a lot more about getting back into school rather than which school I attended.

Unfortunately, we had chosen a Friday to start the enrollment process, and the day had come to an end before we could make our way over to Benjamin Franklin Middle School. My mother could only stay a couple of days, and she was scheduled to return back to New Jersey on Sunday. I would have to finish the enrollment process without her. Sunday morning, my mother slipped away at the break of dawn. She didn't say much of a goodbye, but my brother and I had already accepted our lives without her immediate presence in them. She had left, but this time she left me with something I desperately needed—an opportunity for an education. I had a second chance at school, and I was prepared to make the most out of it.

Now I was ready for my first day of school. School had been stripped away from me, but God gave it right back. I was happy to get on the school bus with other kids my age, but probably even happier to walk through the front doors of the school. The school bus dropped us off in the rear of the school, and I followed the mass of students making their way into the school building. Everything felt so new to me. I had basically been making adult decisions for the past two years, and I had forgotten how to be a kid my age.

I felt a little lost but anxious for my return to school. It might seem a bit odd, but I really didn't know what grade level I was supposed to be and neither did the front office. I made it towards the end of my seventh grade year while I was in Lebanon Middle School, but I never finished the school year when I was there. I wondered which grade level Franklin MS would place me. When I made it inside of the school building, I was instructed to wait in the front office until they figured everything out.

The first week of school was so boring and lifeless because I spent about 95% of it in that front office. Without my mother being present for the rest of the enrollment process, I had to finish the process by myself. It consisted of numerous phone calls to my past schools asking for transcripts and searching for medical records. I was in the office so long that they made me their "office helper" and had me delivering notes and packages to different teachers around the school. I knew the layout of the school before I ever attended any classes. It turned out to be a very good thing that I spent that time in the office, because it allowed me to slowly adjust back to school life.

Returning back to school initially intimidated me. I was at least two years older than everyone, because I had been out of the school environment for two years. I felt like a student that got held back for two years for flunking classes. I felt a little bit out of place like I was being stared at because I was one of the tallest guys there with a deep voice. I just knew that I'd be judged.

I didn't realize that the streets had affected me and had left me a lot colder than I was before. My facial expressions weren't very welcoming, and my body language seemed to be ready for attack at any moment. I was very alert and aware of my surrounding at all times. I had been robbed, jumped, and harassed on the streets, so it left my body and mind in a 24-hour defensive state. My mind was still stuck in street survival mode, and it wasn't an easy mind state to separate from my head. I had come from a tough background and didn't know how the transition back to school life would pan out for me.

Working in the front office helped me slowly ease back into things, and I met my first friend there, a guy by the name of Alan Ortiz.

He asked me, "Why are you always in here? You must have beef with a lot of people if you keep getting sent here?"

I laughed at his joke, and we both proceeded to introduce ourselves. Alan possessed the kind of personality that was really mellow and far from offensive. We built a solid base for a friendship in only a brief exchange of words. That's all it really took back then to start a good friendship.

The first week of school passed by, and I was still waiting in the front office. My family at home kept asking me what was delaying the enrollment process, and I told them that I had no idea. Everyday, I would pack my school bag and be ready for school, but school wasn't ready for me. Finally after a week, the front office had come to a decision that I would be in the 7th grade since I never officially finished the school year in Lebanon MS.

I walked into the front office, and the woman behind the desk said, "I have good news for you. I have your class schedule right here, and you report to your classes today."

She made my morning very special with that news. I had waited over two years for this moment, and finally, it was going to happen. I took my class schedule from her, and she told me that I could go ahead and make my way to my first period class.

When I arrived at my first period class, which was Science, the class was already in session. The classroom door creaked as I slowly opened it and peeked my head inside. This brought more attention to my entrance into the classroom and made it more awkward for me. Everyone in the classroom gazed at the "new kid" and wondered why I was so tall, why my voice was so deep, and if I had flunked a couple of grades. I was sure by the way their eyes locked onto me that these were some of the questions that ran through their heads.

The awkwardness grew when the science teacher, Ms. Jackson, asked me to stand in front and introduce myself to the class. I slowly made my way to the front of the classroom, turned towards the rest of the students, and started to introduce myself.

Ms. Jackson then interrupted my introduction and pointed out to the class, "Wow, you have a really deep voice. Are you sure this is your right class?"

Everyone in the classroom started laughing, and I just smiled and said, "Yes ma'am, that's what my schedule says."

She smiled back and said, "Alright, you'll be sitting next to Alan Ortiz, and he'll be your lab partner for the next six weeks."

Talk about having luck in your favor. I was excited to be paired with a familiar face.

I liked hanging around Alan. Alan was one of the top three "must know" guys in school, and hanging around him automatically made me cool by association. One day I went to the cafeteria for lunch, and I saw the longest lunch line of my life. The line wrapped around the entire cafeteria and was longer than the line at Six Flags. I started making my way to the end of the line, but Alan called me over to him. He was almost at the front of the line, and he said that I could cut in front of him. I thought some people would get mad about it, but once again, Alan was a "must know" guy. He had some pull around the school, and he told everyone that I was with him so no one made a fuss about it. I was very lucky that Alan was the first person I had met at Franklin MS.

Alan is the reason I met my next friend there too. One day while waiting in the cafeteria line, a funny-looking kid came up to Alan skipping everyone else in line. He had big ears, a goofy smile, kind of chubby, with a unibrow that stole the show from the rest of his face.

He came up to us and I said, "Wow, this guy looks like Dewey from *Malcolm in the Middle*."

Alan laughed and said, "Hey Brion, this is one of my good friends Omari. Omari, this is Brion. He's from St. Louis. He's new here."

That name "Omari" may not be worth much now, but it will add value to itself later on in the story.

I met another one of my best friends in a very strange manner. One morning I was nervous because I had lost my school badge the day before. I couldn't find my badge anywhere, and the school was very strict about having the school badge visible at all times of the day. Students who did not have a badge received a "write up" that could turn into a referral for disciplinary action. I decided to head to the school office that morning with the hope that someone had turned in my badge.

While I was heading towards the office, I saw a kid talking to one of the administrators in the hallway. He was a thin kid with a mini afro.

The administrator then pointed towards me and said, "That's his badge."

I could not believe this kid tried to steal my badge and thought he was going to get away with it. I was so upset that this imposter tried to use my badge. He claimed later on in life that he had picked up the badge off of the floor, because he thought it was his badge. He said he took it home, his mom then noticed that it wasn't his badge while she was doing laundry, and he decided to turn in the badge to the office the next day. He said he was speaking to the administrator and asking her if she knew who this kid was on the badge, and then that's when I walked by in the hallway. He had his story, but I'm still sticking to mine. I write this story with as much sarcasm and humility as possible, because we still jokingly debate this incident at least once a year.

When I went to the basketball court that day, I noticed that the same guy who "stole my badge" was now hanging around us. I asked Alan about the thief's name since Alan knew everyone in school.

Alan said, "Oh him? That's Kevin."

Then I pointed to a taller kid standing next to him and a shorter kid talking to Kevin.

Alan said, "The tall one is Steven and the shorter one is Galen. We've all been good friends for a long time."

These kids eventually became my best friends in life. It was more than friendship. It was the start of a brotherhood. I'm proud to say that I've been best friends with these same guys for more than 13 years now.

The reason I include these guys in the story, is due to their importance in my life. I had no luck making friends before them. They gave me the friendship that I had always wanted. They became my family. They became my brothers. They showed me the true meaning of friendship. Without knowing it, I became their leader. This was always weird to me because I never considered myself in that role. Everyone else did. I just stood up for what I believed in and made sure no one messed with anyone in our group. I guess you could say my job was the protector.

Our group quickly rose from six members to about thirty, and my name became well known around school. I wanted to form a group that people could join and just be themselves and not feel pressured to be someone they're not in order to be accepted. Most of the members in the group were scared of the other "tough guy" groups in school because they were afraid they would be picked on and bullied. I wouldn't have any of that "bullying" stuff going on while I was around. I could never just sit back and watch one of my friends get bullied. I stood up for my friends more times than I can remember.

I had to earn respect around the school by making alliances and stepping to some scary-looking dudes. Before I knew it, no one would bother the "nerds" in my group because they knew who protected those guys. In a sense, I had become just like my big brother Justin.

I even had one of the guys in my group come to me and say, "Brion, I like you as our leader. I have a lot of respect for you."

Guys from the "tough guy" groups told me this as well. I didn't know where I had gotten my demeanor as someone who deserved respect, because my brother claimed he never had as much respect that I acquired from others. He didn't only mean just from other people, but he also meant internal respect.

Justin told me, "You are a very respectful kid. You probably got it from Ma."

Maybe it was from him or maybe it was from my mother. Wherever I got the respect attribute from, it was working out for me and causing my group of friends to multiply on a daily basis.

I didn't really know I had a "crew" until I went up to a girl at lunch and she said, "Wow, Brion, did you really have to bring your whole posse to come see me?"

I turned around and there were about twenty guys standing there waiting for me.

Steven then stepped up and said, "So, are we going to play basketball or what?"

I had no other choice but to smile.

I stared at them and I said, "Yeah. One sec." I then turned back towards the girl and said, "These are my brothers. We go everywhere together."

I had transitioned from having no friends and being bullied in St. Louis to now having a whole crew who looked up to me as their brother.

People always told me that it's really hard for them to believe that I didn't have any friends growing up in St. Louis, and I tell them that people back in St. Louis would find it very hard to believe that I have friends now. People also told me that I always had a constant group around me that was hanging onto every word I said, though I never noticed it. I just liked telling stories about my upbringing and bringing light to dark times. I liked to entertain people and make them laugh. I guess I didn't want anyone to feel the pain that I felt inside from my past. When I see others laughing and smiling in a good atmosphere, it makes me do the same. I love people, and I'm even happier when they love me back.

So, I was now back in school, doing fairly well academically, had a solid group of friends, and I also talked to my mother on the phone more often than I did before. Everything seemed as though it was going smoothly in my life, but it wasn't that way at the house. My brother and I had gotten our own apartment in the same apartment complex as my cousin Jordan. My brother's girlfriend and her daughter also moved in with us to the new apartment. She was the same woman who had kicked me and my brother out of her house the first time I met her, so I wasn't too thrilled about her staying with us. We had our ups and downs, but she stayed. We now had more people in the house to care for each day. The money in the house would quickly deplete, and my brother and I would go on the hunt for bringing food into the house.

Since food was a constant struggle in our home, school breakfasts and lunches became a "must have" on a daily basis. The school definitely wasn't serving five-star lunches, but I wasn't in much of a position to complain. As long as the food was edible, I was the first in line. I made sure I was present at school each day for the free breakfast and free lunch. Even with the school lunches, I was still hungry. I was a growing teenager, and my appetite had grown with me. I was a poor kid whose stomach growled louder than the rational thoughts in my brain.

It was difficult to get food for our apartment since my brother struggled to find a job. My brother had a job every now and again, but he struggled to maintain one for any lengthy amount of time. I still don't know to this day where or when he ate, but he somehow found a way. He would randomly surprise me some mornings by bringing a sausage and biscuit sandwich for me to eat. Those were the good mornings.

While living with my brother in that apartment, I had complete freedom. Even with that freedom, I never abused it. I respected my brother too much to stay out all hours of the night. I felt after a certain time of the night, there was nothing but trouble waiting out in the streets. I was usually in the house before dark doing homework. Maybe I was just a weird kid, or maybe I just grew past those things when "fast forward" was pressed on my childhood. I had possessed the ability to do what I wanted for years, but I just chose not to do wrong. It was my choice and I liked it. To this day, I don't regret not doing the bad things I could've done. I was often told that I was an 80-year-old man trapped inside of a 14-year-old body. I was a homebody that enjoyed the simple activities inside.

My friend Omari felt bad that I didn't have at least a game station at my place. He was confused about how I spent all of this time at home, but I didn't have a videogame system. We were too poor to buy one, so Omari promised that I could have his old Playstation 2 (PS2) since he had just bought the slim version of the PS2. Omari's mother, who didn't have much knowledge about me at the time, thought I was just using him to get his PS2. She told him that I'd be gone out of his life as soon as I got the PS2 in my hands.

Luckily, Omari didn't believe the hype his mother tried to say about me. He gave me the PS2 and told me that we were friends who would always have each other's backs. I was grateful for what he had done.

Time went by, and my friendship with Omari grew with each passing month. Omari's mother even admitted that she was wrong about me and embraced me into their family. They were from Kurdistan. Omari lived with his mom, and his older sister. Omari's sister was drop-dead gorgeous.

Her name was Rowan (Wan for short). I loved Wan. I loved Wan because she loved me. She was a year older than my brother. Some days, I would be starving at my house with nothing in our fridge but baking soda. When it was time for me to leave Omari's house and return home, Wan would volunteer to take me home and stop by any fast food place she thought was my favorite.

I remember one time I hadn't eaten in days, but when Wan asked me, "Brion, are you hungry?" I said, "No."

I don't know why I said no. I guess I said it because I didn't want to inconvenience her or put my burdens on her. I'd rather starve than bring my problems onto anyone else, but Wan was a very persistent woman. She got past my stubbornness every time. She pulled up to a fast food drive thru anyway. The back and forth match between us shortly began afterwards.

Wan asked me, "So, what do you want to eat?"

And I said, "I'm not hungry."

Then she said, "Okay, if you were hungry, what would you get?"

I responded, "I don't know, because my body isn't hungry."

Wan said, "Okay, I'm hungry. Could you choose something for me to eat?"

Then I just stared at her, because I was on short supply of witty responses. Due to her getting the best of me in the back and forth match, I had to resort to my last line of defense—absolute silence.

She grew tired of my silence and said, "Brion, there's cars behind us and we're not leaving this spot until you choose something to eat, so you better choose quickly."

I was just thinking in my head like, "She has to be bluffing right now. There's no way she'd do something like that."

Wan then stared at me and turned off the car while we were sitting in the front of the drive-thru line. The cars behind us immediately started honking and becoming agitated, but Wan didn't budge. She just crossed her arms and stared at me. When she did that, I knew I had lost the battle, so I ordered something to eat. Wan then smiled at me, and I asked her to just get me the small combo meal.

She said, "Okay," and then turned to the speaker to order and said, "Yeah, I'll take the large combo and add extra everything if you can." Wan then handed me my bag of food and drink, and then smiled at me again and said, "Brion, must we do this every time?"

Wan dropped me off at my house, and I told her thank you. She would always say that I didn't have to say thank you, but I always did.

I was very courteous with the food Wan had bought me until I got into the house, and then I was like a monster with it. I quickly scarfed the food down. I was so happy for the food Wan had bought me, and my stomach was even more grateful for the meal. That food didn't even have a chance against my hunger. Wan was very kind-hearted, and she was an all-around great person. I was too young to marry her at the time so I had to keep my options open.

While I was focused on bettering my relationship with Omari and his family, my brother was focused on adding new additions to our family. My brother eventually had one child with his girlfriend, and now she was pregnant with number two. Our apartment now held my brother, his girlfriend, her daughter, my niece, and one baby on the way. Thankfully, we had moved to a two-bedroom apartment in another apartment complex, so I had my own room. I was happy that I finally had my own space after years of sleeping on the couch and the floor.

Everything was good until one day after shortly moving into the apartment, my brother told me that my nieces would be getting my room, and I would be taking the couch. This upset me a lot. I had finally gotten my own room and now it was being taken away from me. I couldn't stand the thought of having no privacy and no room to call my own, so I moved into the walk-in coat closet. I didn't want to be bothered by the world at times, and it was the only place I could go to escape troubles I had in my life. It brought me peace.

My grandma came to visit one day from St. Louis, and she was very upset that my room was a closet while everyone else had their own rooms. She didn't like it, but I assured my grandmother that I've had worse places to sleep and I'd be fine. Yes, this was the same grandmother that put me out in the past. I had learned to forgive her within my heart by this time in my life. I held no grudges against anyone. I always felt that those people who I held grudges against were moving on with their lives, and I was stuck within mine trying to blame them for everything. So instead of carrying negative energy with me, I forgave them all. My brother didn't have those same feelings about forgiveness at the time. He chose to hold those people accountable for the crimes they committed. We clearly had two different mindsets.

Yes, I lived in a closet, I was hungry about 80% of the time, but I was thankful. I had my health, good friends, and I was in school. To me, I was blessed. I always thought to myself that there was someone out there in the world who had worse circumstances than me. I wanted to make the best out of the life I had, because I knew that it could all change at any second.

So it came as no surprise that one day after school, I returned home, and the front door to our apartment was locked. I tried my house key, and it still didn't open. I then looked at the notice on the door, which I had seen over a million times before. The notice on the door read "Notice of Eviction." I was locked out, and all of my belongings were inside. In my head, I had just lost my peace of sanity, my area to retreat back to from the world, and now we were being evicted yet again and forced to restart.

At this point in my life I was mentally exhausted. I always tell people to try and imagine hitting the reset button on your life every time you start to make progress. What made matters worse was that I didn't have control of when the reset button would be hit. It was a surprise to me each time.

I called my brother, and he told me that he and his girlfriend were going to check out some houses to move to next. He asked me if I could find somewhere to stay until they figure out the living situation. Who other than Omari could I think of? I called him and told him what happened, and he told me to come over so we could devise a plan. We were two teenagers sitting in his living room devising a living plan for my life.

By this time, I had been coming to Omari's house almost every single weekend for months. I never told him, but his house was my escape. When I was in his house, it gave me a chance to just have fun and not worry about someone breaking into my house, shooting outside my house, eviction notices on the door, or worrying about what I was going to eat for the day. His house was my little taste of heaven I got once a week. Omari's mom was used to me and Kevin's presence at her home, but this was different. It was usually the three of us, but not this day. It was just Omari and I devising the plan.

Omari said that he would ask his mom if I could spend the night every night until she started noticing that I still hadn't returned home. Yep, that's where hours of planning got us. Maybe the videogames we were playing while talking about our plan greatly affected the end result. Even though it wasn't the best plan in the world, we stuck with it and put the plan into action.

Omari kept asking his mom each night if I could stay, and his mom agreed. She soon caught on to our plan, but I still ended up staying about two weeks. She knew what was happening, but she didn't complain. She only embraced me more into the family. She said I was the big brother that Omari always needed. I would give him his daily "big brother beat down" sessions (the same ones my brother gave to me growing up), and then we'd spend the rest of the day messing stuff up around the house.

His mom would always say, "Brion, we're going to have to build you a room here."

I'm still waiting for that room to this day, but she always made me feel welcome in her home.

Staying with Omari and his family made me question my family back in my hometown. They did something that my own blood family in Lebanon wouldn't do for me. This family had no ties to me but welcomed me into their home. In my eyes, Omari, his mom and his sister were my family. They had given me a place to live when I had nowhere else to go, fed me when I had nothing else to eat, and gave me clothes when I had nothing else to wear. They knew I couldn't repay them, but they helped anyway. I didn't know what the true definition of a family was, but I knew it looked a lot like theirs. We had our quarrels, but it always ended with apologies at the end of the day and lots of hugs. It may sound cheesy, but I liked that feeling. I was proud to say that they were my family. I stayed with them until my brother called me and said that he had found a place for us to live in South Dallas. I packed my bags, thanked Omari's family for everything, and they dropped me off at my new home.

* * *

I met this other kid named Davis on the Franklin MS basketball team. We were the Franklin Falcons. Our school basketball team consisted of Omari, Kevin, Galen, Davis, and me. They all knew Davis, but I didn't know him. I wasn't planning on knowing him either. Davis and I had bad blood that started from Algebra class. I didn't like him, and he didn't like me. Neither of us remembers exactly why we didn't like each other, but we knew the dislike of one another definitely existed at the beginning. We both initially judged each other without knowing each other's true background. We planned on not talking to each other and gave evil looks each time we crossed paths in the hallway, but the basketball team changed all of that.

On the basketball team, we were forced to work together and talk to one another. We had no other choice but to become close and figure things out. Slowly, Davis and I started becoming good friends. We found out more about each other and realized we actually had a lot more in common than we thought. We started hanging out together at school, and Davis even invited me over his house one day, which has a story within itself.

I lived in the "hood" at this time, and Davis lived in a very "well-to-do" neighborhood. I walked many miles over to his house and didn't have any trouble until I made it to his neighborhood. I was walking with my backpack filled with my basketball gear, because we had planned on playing basketball at his house.

While I was walking to his house, a police officer pulled up next to me and said, "Hey buddy, can I talk to you for a second?"

I thought that maybe it was just to ask me some simple routine question, but he told me to stop walking. The officer picked up his radio and whispered something into it.

I heard him tell his police radio, "Yeah, I got him."

I heard this and started panicking in my head about what was going on. The cop was a white male, heavyset, and bald.

The cop got out of his car and asked, "Where are you headed to?"

I responded, "To my friend's house."

He then said, "Oh really? Where does your friend live?"

I had never been over to Davis's house before, and I could only remember the first part of the street name since it was a weird street name.

So I responded, "It's like Pem—something."

The cop then said, "Yeah, okay."

Now, you have to remember that my last encounter with a cop was getting hit over the head and pushed by Officer Burt, so I was taking this pretty well even though I had bad feelings about cops at this time. I still tried to remain calm and respectful.

He then went on and said, "Well, I'm gonna get straight to the point. We've been getting a lot of calls saying a suspicious bla.... male is walking through the neighborhood."

He started to say the word "black" in that statement, but then stopped and just said "male."

I was a very level-headed kid and just simply responded with, "Oh."

Then he asked, "What's in the backpack?"

I said, "My basketball gear."

He then asked me, "Mind if I check?"

I responded, "Yes, I do mind, because I just told you it was my basketball gear."

The cop became agitated that I wouldn't let him check it, and said, "Well, why don't you hurry up and get to where you're going to. You have a good day."

I started walking away and said, "Yeah, right. You too."

I didn't know I had to rush to get to a destination. I felt like I was being harassed. I didn't want to let that cop ruin my day, so I focused on making it to my friend's house.

I finally made it to Davis's house and rang the doorbell. I looked at the end of the street and saw the sign that said "Pemberton." I had gotten the first part of the street name right. While I'm listening to the dogs bark from inside the house, I looked down the street and saw the same police officer slowly driving down the street towards me. The same police officer who had stopped me just minutes beforehand, had followed me to Davis's house. I no longer "felt" like I was being harassed. I knew I was being harassed. I waved at him with a big fake smile. He waved back with the same smile, put his car in park and waited a few houses down from me in his police squad car facing Davis's house.

Finally, Davis's mom opened the door, and her exact response when she opened the door was, "Sorry, we don't want any. Thank you anyway" and then closed the door.

I was shocked. It's important to know that Davis's mom had never seen me before, but she didn't even give me a chance to say anything. She just closed the door. She thought I was trying to sell her something. Her quick action to close the door provoked the officer to mouth something into his police radio and start to get out of the car.

Before the officer could take two steps towards me, Davis's mom then opened the door again and said, "Oh wait, are you here for Davis? You're one of his friends aren't you? I'm so sorry!"

The cop then stopped midstride with a puzzled look on his face and got back into his car as I went inside of the house. I heard a knock at the door when I greeted Davis in his room, but I never asked about who was there. I wouldn't be surprised if it was the same police officer.

Instead of making a big commotion about the incident, I simply told Davis, "Dang bro, security is tight in your neighborhood."

That was the only time I mentioned the officer that day. I never let bad moments or bad people ruin my day. I spent the rest of the day with Davis having fun, and we eventually became best friends.

For every week I wasn't with Omari and Kevin, I was with Davis. We were either playing in basketball tournaments together or just hanging out doing something fun. Our friendship grew, and Davis's family became my family. Davis's family was always nice to me like Omari's family. They made sure I ate and always kept up with what I was doing in my life. They guaranteed me a ride home at the end of the day so I wouldn't have to walk. Yet my friendship with Davis did more than that—Davis led me to a church that was very beneficial to my life.

Davis asked me one day while we were hanging out, "Hey, do you want to come to youth group with me one night at my church?"

I asked him, "What's that all about?"

He said, "It's this thing we do at my church in the evening time. It's pretty fun. You should come."

I told him, "Well, that sounds pretty lame, but I'll go anyway."

The day I attended the youth group service with Davis started another chapter in my life. Lovers Lane United Methodist Church was a turning point. Davis got me into the very church that I would soon grow to love. I had agreed to attend the youth group, and my journey continued.

CHAPTER 6:

GOING AGAINST THE ODDS

B y this time Davis and I had gotten closer and our friendship had reached a new height. Davis had just asked me to go to church with him, but I wasn't too excited to go. I believed in God and was seeing more and more of his work within my life every day, but I just didn't want to return to the church setting. I mean my clothes were a bit better, but I felt that they weren't "church better." I hadn't been to church in a long time, and I was concerned about people judging me.

It was a very common thing for people to judge others at the previous churches I had attended. Everyone would just stare at anyone who looked a bit different or weren't the most put together, and instead of helping them, they'd just talk about them. Growing up, my own family were some of those very critics, and I didn't want to be a part of it. But since I had already promised Davis I would go, I decided to keep my promise and attend the service.

Davis said he didn't want to just throw me into his main church, so we went to a small group meeting first. Small groups happened in the evening time, and it was a place where teenagers around the same age could all get together in a controlled environment and have conversations about God. The first time I attended the small group at Davis's church was not the best. The kids in the group spent most of the time talking about the football game (which I didn't watch at all) or discussing random things that had absolutely nothing to do with church. I found this very odd, and I didn't really like it.

Around the last five minutes of the meeting, however, everyone in the youth group got really serious, and we had a real discussion about our faiths. I really enjoyed this part of the meeting, because my faith was being discovered and I really wanted to hear the testimonies of other people who were also struggling to find their walk of faith. Those last five minutes were the absolute reason I didn't walk out. I was happy that I made that decision to stay, because things got a lot better after that.

The church served dinner to all of the small groups, and they let us play sports in the gym after we were done. While we were walking to the room that served dinner, I met the main youth pastor, Grant Myers. Before you could eat, you had to give five dollars at the door. I was living in the hood with no money and barely getting food, so that five dollars was completely out of the question for me. Because I couldn't afford the dinner, I decided to just go back to the gym and play basketball.

I started walking to the gym, but Pastor Grant stopped me and said, "Hey, go eat. Your dinner is on me."

My previous churches hadn't done anything like this before, and I was extremely grateful. He even let me take home some of the leftover boxes of pizza. When I brought home the pizza, it was like a Christmas miracle, because everyone got a chance to eat in the house. Nothing created a better feeling inside of me than seeing my whole family eat.

I started going to small groups more and more, but I was still having some trouble transitioning into the group. Davis told me to come to the morning youth worship service, because there would be more teenagers around our age. I decided to attend the service, knowing that I had to confront my fears of being judged at church. I tried to maintain a positive outlook, but when I first stepped foot into the service, I felt like the odd man out. Everyone just gave me stares, but no one spoke to me. I tailed Davis wherever he went and watched him greet his friends in the service.

The service was great and I liked the way Grant preached, but I didn't feel connected to the group. I didn't have that sense of belonging that I was hoping for. Instead, I had the sense of disconnection and things only got worse with time. I tried telling myself that people aren't talking to me because I'm the new guy and that'll change with time, but it didn't.

After about a month or so of going to the church, my only friend was still Davis. I felt alone at the church, and I started to feel like I didn't belong there. I told the youth pastor after service one day that I would not be returning.

Pastor Grant looked at me and said, "Whoa, okay. I understand what you're saying, but I got a deal for you. There's this youth trip coming up pretty soon called the Back to School Retreat at Sky Ranch, and I want you to go on it. Don't worry about paying for anything. If after the trip you still decide to leave the church, then you can leave with no questions asked. Deal?"

I thought about it for a second and then said, "Deal."

I agreed to the deal because I knew there was no way that some weekend trip would change my mind. I felt strongly about not going back to church, and nothing was going to change that...or so I thought. The trip seemed like it could be fun, but I felt like it wasn't for me since I didn't really know anyone other than Davis.

The church did this thing on the youth trip where they would hang up individual posters on the walls with each youth group member's name on it. The idea of the posters was to let the kids on the trip sign their friend's posters with a positive message. It was similar to a yearbook. During the trip, I saw tons of people go around signing posters, so I wanted to check mine to see who had wrote on it. I wasn't surprised to find that only the church counselors, Davis, and Davis' twin sisters had written something on it. I was a bit disappointed, but I kind of expected it.

I had decided to not hang around Davis too much on the trip. I wanted him to be able to have his own personal time to hang out with his other friends. I didn't want him to feel obligated to hang out with me because he was my only friend there. I decided to do my own thing, so I walked off and headed to the basketball court at Sky Ranch.

Basketball had become my favorite sport at this time. My favorite basketball player was and still is, LeBron James. I liked basketball because it was a sport I was becoming better at, and it was something I knew I had a good chance of winning at if I played. When I made it to the basketball court, there was another kid playing there. I didn't know it at the time, but I was about to meet my next best friend.

I walked up to him and introduced myself, and he said his name was Jake Mwangi. He was another basketball player at the church who loved the game, and he also felt he could beat everyone he played against. I liked the passion he had inside of him about winning, and I felt that I should be the one to beat him and humble him a bit. We both agreed to play a friendly game of one on one to see who was the better basketball player.

We played hard against each other and at the time, I didn't know Jake was a huge trash talker and a rage monster when it came to basketball. I ended up beating Jake five games in a row in the hot

Texas sun, but he refused to quit. He just kept asking for more re-matches, and he started getting more upset with each loss.

He said, "We're not leaving until I win!"

I felt bad that Jake couldn't beat me, so I slacked off one of the games and let him win. I was physically exhausted, and I had hoped that letting him win would end all of the never-ending matches. Even with the win, Jake took his anger outside of the basketball court and stormed off to dinner.

While we were walking to dinner, Jake, who was very known at the church and well liked, passed a couple of girls from our church heading to the dinner hall at Sky Ranch.

The girls saw that Jake was upset and turned around to me and said, "What did you do to Jake?! Why are you even here at our church? This is why no one will talk to you!"

I was deeply hurt by the girls' words, but I had heard worse and endured a lot more in my time. I just shrugged off the comments without saying a word, and I went into isolation. That was my defense mechanism when it came to anything that disturbed me or irritated me. If someone didn't want me around, I simply disappeared.

After showering from basketball, I walked outside of the cabin and three girls approached me. I thought they were a part of the girl group from earlier that said those hurtful comments to me, but they were different. They came and asked me if I wanted to walk to the dinner hall with them. They said their names were Virginia, Jacky, and Melissa. I liked them, because they actually engaged in a conversation with me.

I remember telling them that I was very antisocial and that I was a very boring person. I told them these things, but they didn't buy it. They kept laughing at the things I said, and they told me that I was funny and very far from antisocial. The truth was simple: I wanted to meet people, but I wasn't too sure they wanted to meet me.

There were mostly rich kids at the church, and I had gotten teased and bullied many times when I tried to hang out with kids like that in the past. I was sure their image of me was negative, but these three were different. These girls gave my mind a whole new perspective towards the retreat trip. The "tres amigas" and I went everywhere together on that trip. They honestly made the trip more enjoyable, because I finally had other people to hang out with besides Davis.

The church counselors had every student on the trip write their names onto a piece of paper. Then they put the pieces of paper into a big bucket, and each student had to draw out someone's name and introduce himself or herself to that person. They had to find out things about the person they chose and converse with the person. The whole point of the game was for people to talk to someone that they wouldn't normally talk to at church, but the game concept tremendously failed.

People were looking at the names and taking sneak peeks while choosing the names they wanted to draw. I stuck to the rules and drew someone's name at random. I drew the name, but I didn't even bother to open it up and read it. I decided that no random person was really interested in talking to me anyway, so why bother? I balled the paper up and put it in my pants pocket.

That same night, everyone in the youth group went stargazing, except the cool kids who felt stargazing was dumb. I was the kid who was actually intrigued by the whole thing. I had never been able to see so many stars before, but that night, I saw them all. It was an experience that was very much worthwhile. I was simply amazed by the beauty of the stars. I never realized that the world extended so far beyond what my eyes could see. Each star I saw gave testimony to life that had the potential to extend far beyond myself.

I remember sitting next to Melissa and a youth group mentor, the legendary Gary. I started talking to Gary and Melissa about the beauty of the stars, and I pointed out familiar constellations I had learned about in school. We roasted marshmallows around the campfire, shared stories, and had deep conversations about the universe. I pretty much spent the whole night with Gary and Melissa.

After the campfire, I returned back to the cabin and started changing into my clothes for bed. When I folded my pants, I noticed I had a piece of paper in my pocket. It was the same piece of paper from earlier in the day with a name on it. I unfolded the piece of paper and looked at the name on it. To my surprise, the name on the paper said "Melissa Gregory." The same Melissa I had spent the whole day with doing activities. That was the strangest thing to me. I didn't want to participate in the activity, but I ended up participating in the activity anyway. Go figure. Here was another reason why I don't believe in coincidences.

Towards the end of the trip, all of the students went to the worship hall to hear Pastor Grant preach. Pastor Grant gave a sermon to the entire youth group that dealt with the topic of "forgiveness." The name of the youth group was "Inside Out." I didn't understand why Pastor Grant chose that name, but he later made it clear to all of us.

He said, "We believe that we must first change ourselves on the inside before we are able to go out and help the world."

While he was on stage preaching, I zoned out in my head and went into a different world. I started thinking about my uncle who had choked me, my grandma who threw me out, my family who had turned their backs to me in my time of need, starvation, poverty, my mom leaving us, and all sorts of things that happened to me in my past. In the midst of all of these thoughts, I just said to myself, "I forgive you."

I don't know where those words came from, but I knew it had to be from somewhere deep inside of me. Then I started questioning myself, which actually made things clearer for me.

I started wondering what holding grudges against people actually did. It solved nothing. It just put a ton of hate in my heart that I didn't want to be there. I didn't want future people like Jacky and Virginia, or anyone else I encountered to pay for the mistakes of the people that came before them. I didn't think that was fair at all. Why hold hate? Why look down on the people who looked down on you? I didn't want to do the wrongs that they did to me. If I wanted my life to be better I knew I had to start off by changing myself on the inside first.

It had to start with true forgiveness. Not for them, but for myself. I had been filled with hate and anger from the things I had experienced up to that point. I envisioned my uncle and his hands clasped around my neck, and I started to cry a little.

I said to myself, "I forgive you. There is no hatred against you in my heart."

I said this in a quiet voice, and the weird thing is, I meant it. I thought to myself that he was able to go to sleep each night without feeling bad, or maybe he did, but I also wanted to be able to go to sleep each night, so I forgave him. Just like that, I felt a bit better, so I continued.

I thought about every situation in my past and just said, "I forgive you," and I even gave reasoning behind it.

I thought about the kids bullying me throughout the years and said, "You were only kids. You didn't know any better. I can't hold that against you. Who you were is not always who you will become. I forgive you."

I couldn't let those people hold me back from making new friends and meeting great people in the world. I went on forgiving everyone in my life, and then it came to my mom. I just smiled. That's all I could do.

Even though I was crushed by her absence and completely heartbroken by her actions, I couldn't hold anything against her. I just thought to myself about everything she had ever done in my life to ensure it was perfect before she ever left. I remembered her working nonstop overtimes at her job so my brother and I could have the things she missed out on as a kid. She always made sure we had somewhere to sleep and something to eat, and told us she loved us dearly every single night. The people who judged my mom and called her an unfit mother made me very upset.

I always said, "You judge her by her actions because that's all you know of her, but we know who she truly is inside. We knew who she was before she left us."

I didn't feel that it was right to judge someone like that. Not just because it was my mother, but also because it just felt wrong to me.

People would say, "I can't see how she just left y'all like that. I would never leave my kids."

I answered, "Hey, neither would my mother."

She loved us just as much as anyone else who has kids, so it was very confusing to us when she left. It was something out of the ordinary.

I continued to connect to Pastor Grant's sermon at the retreat.

I also continued thinking about my mother and said to myself, "You are lost and I will not hold that against you, but I will pray for the day you find yourself again and return as my mother."

I realized that she made a mistake, and I tried to put myself into her shoes.

I started thinking, "How must she feel right now? She must be utterly destroyed inside. Why didn't she return sooner? How could she after doing what she did? I don't know if I would've been able to show my face around town if I had done something like that. But she returned anyway and signed me into school. She faced shame, dirty looks, judgment, and just about everything else. She knew she'd encounter this, but she came back anyway and signed me up into the place I loved and needed to be."

I then opened my eyes and said, "I forgive you all, and I love you."

I told you that I was an 80-year-old man trapped in a teenager's body. I had prayed to God for wisdom, and I felt like I was receiving that gift. My maturity had grown at that point, and that was the day I had discovered the true meaning of forgiveness and understanding. I was very old in my mind, and that would prove to be a positive in the future.

Pastor Grant ended his sermon for the day, but I had just begun mine inside. I could only smile. I had changed my feelings inside, and it was starting to change the way I appeared on the outside. That "cold look" I had developed from living on the streets slowly started to vanish. It started to change my mannerisms and the way acted. I felt like I had newfound energy in life. I was starting to like this youth group. I knew at that moment that this was my church—Inside Out ministry was mine.

* * *

I returned home after a very good ending to the youth trip. I briefed my brother on everything that had occurred, and he was happy that I had found a church. I told Justin about the forgiveness I had found inside of myself. He was happy for me, but it wasn't so easy for him to understand. Justin couldn't see a way he could forgive those people in the past who hurt us.

While speaking with my brother, I learned another lesson that day. Everyone is different, and not everyone has instant forgiveness in their hearts. For some, it takes a lot longer than others. Justin felt that he would eventually forgive everyone one day, but in his own time. As much as I wanted my brother to forgive everyone at that moment, I knew it would take some time.

I was now in the 8th grade at Benjamin Franklin Middle School. My group at school, along with its new members, started talking about which high schools they were going to attend. They were acting like we were on our way to college or something. They all started stressing out and panicking about which high school would be the best option and if we would ever see each other again. I reassured them that we'd be fine, but in truth, I didn't really know. There were rumors going around school that the school district board members were talking about changing the jurisdiction lines again. My group eventually decided that we'd all go to Hillcrest High School (or "Hoodcrest" in some neighborhoods). I was relieved to know that we would all still be together in high school and that everything would be perfect, but then one teacher had to ruin everything.

I had a lot of teachers at Franklin MS who actually cared about what happened to their students outside of the classrooms unlike my past schools. I wish I could name them individually, but I don't want any teachers finding me who didn't get their name mentioned in this book. On one particular day, my history teacher came up to me and hassled me about applying to what I called, "The School for Nerds."

She had been hassling me for weeks at a time saying, "Brion please apply! I know you're set on Hillcrest High School, but please reconsider. I know you'd be perfect for this school. It's called Townview Magnet High School. You gotta make this decision for yourself and not for your friends."

I kept saying no, but then she offered me extra credit in her History class if I applied. She had always been a tough teacher on me and constantly held me to a very high standard. Even when I would do something right, she would tell me indirectly that I could've done more. Of course, she told me later on that I was a brilliant kid who needed to be challenged and pushed past my limits. When she offered that extra credit, I immediately applied to Townview with very little intention of actually attending the school. I really just applied to get the extra credit in her class.

Townview received my application and actually liked my grades and my personality on paper, so they wrote me back. The only problem was that I never got the letter. My brother and I were bouncing around homes so much that Townview ended up sending the letter to an old address.

Meanwhile, weeks had gone by and I hadn't received anything from Townview. I took it as a sign that they weren't interested in me. Another student who had received their acceptance letter told me that the interviews were scheduled for today, so I called the school to ask them about my letter.

The school said, "Sir, we sent the letter a long while back, and it looks like your interview is supposed to be today at 4:30 pm."

My heart stopped. There were so many worries that passed through my mind that I just froze. The first problem was how I was actually going to make it to the interview. I had no form of transportation and neither did my brother. Second problem was time. Our school let out at 3:30pm, so how was I supposed to make it there by 4:30pm? Even if I caught the public bus, which was my only form of transportation, I still wouldn't make it. My third problem was doubt. I had doubt that even if I went there for the essay and the interview, I felt like I wouldn't make it. I would've wasted my time going all the way out there just to get turned down. I concluded that I wasn't going to go. I'd just go to Hillcrest and be happy with that.

One of my teachers, who for the sake of this story will be Ms. Green, had always been there for me. Ms. Green would listen to the problems I was having at home with food, my living situation and anything else I had to gripe about in life. She would always try to find the positive light of it. She was relatively new herself at Franklin MS, so she could understand most of what I was going through at the time.

Ms. Green also played a big part in me applying to Townview. It was a combo effect of her advice alongside my history teacher's extra credit offer. I had a discussion with Ms. Green one day about wanting to go to Hillcrest instead of Townview, and she had her own opinion on the subject matter. She lectured me about making my own choices in life and not choosing a place just because my friends were going there. My history teacher had also tried to explain that to me, but Ms. Green did a much better job breaking the subject matter down. I don't know why, but I always listened to Ms. Green. Ms. Green was down to earth, and I just felt like she was actually talking to me and not at me.

I had concluded that I wasn't going to Townview, but Ms. Green wasn't having it.

She asked me, "Why are you not going to Townview anymore?"

I responded, "I don't have a ride out there to the interview, and it's almost 3:30pm now. Besides, I'm going to Hillcrest anyway."

Ms. Green looked at me and said, "Never settle for less. I'll take you. Let's go."

I couldn't believe it. At that point in my life I was absolutely lost. It seemed like every time I came to a dead end, something always happened to open the path right back up. God always has a way for his plan to work. It was almost like someone was watching over me.

She then repeated herself, and I said, "Sure."

Ms. Green drove me to Townview before four o'clock even hit. I ended up being the first one there. Before Ms. Green dropped me off, she gave me a mild speech about thinking for myself and doing what's best to better my life.

She told me, "Be yourself. They'll like who you are." And she drove away.

I turned around and looked at this school, and I was amazed by its appearance. The school had a long stone brick walkway, a solid brown color, and looked like an official government building. Townview had the look and feel of a school that meant business. Townview housed the #1 and #2 schools academically in the nation at the time, which was a huge deal. Here I was trying to be a part of that history. Townview was a place that was known for its academic excellence, and I knew that if I got into the school, my mind would get boggled.

Ms. Green later admitted that she wanted me to go to a school that challenged me mentally so I would keep my mind on the books and not let the pressures of other things get in my way. Ms. Green said she knew that I was a bright kid and she would be crushed if anything stopped me from achieving anything shorter than greatness. She told me that and so did a handful of other teachers at Franklin MS. I thought about all the teachers who had high hopes for me, my cousins back in St. Louis rooting for me, Davis's family,

Omari's family, and my mother in New Jersey that had raised me to fight for the dreams that I wanted in life. I felt like I had a lot of people in my corner who all wanted to see me achieve greatness in life. I just knew at that very moment that I HAD to get into Townview.

I was the first student to enter the testing room. I had applied to Townview Law Magnet (Now Judge Barefoot Sanders Law Magnet). When I arrived, a girl, who I believed to be a senior at the school, handed me a piece of paper, a pen and a small prompt. Townview didn't have a clue at the time, but they asked me to do something I actually excelled at—writing.

Life had given me a lot to write about in such a short time. One of the administrators entered the room and stated that it was a timed essay. I believe the prompt was "Why do you want to go here?" This prompt was so easy to answer, because I knew what I had to do in life. I wrote about the people who stuck their necks out for me in the past to ensure I made it to this point in life. I wrote about my brother inspiring me everyday to continue fighting no matter what happened to us. And finally, I wrote about wanting to achieve more in life and never settling for less. I felt like Townview was that next step in my journey. While I was finishing my essay, other applicants started to arrive in the room by the dozens. My time finally ran out as an administrator made their way up to me and took my essay from me.

He then said, "It's time for the interview now."

After my feeling of nervousness and nausea passed, I walked into the interview room and saw two old men sitting behind a table with the same senior girl that I had seen at the door. They told me to take a seat in front of them, and the interview began.

The interview was like a drill session. Questions were being thrown from all angles, but I had a response for everything. I continued answering everything until the interview was finally over.

One of the old men, Mr. Lewis, leaned forward and said, "I can't officially say this on paper yet, but welcome to Townview."

After hearing those words, I almost passed out in my seat. I couldn't believe they actually wanted me to be a part of their school. My eyes grew big with excitement as I listened for his next words.

Mr. Lewis continued, "It's hard for any of us to say no to you. I've only known you for a few minutes and can already tell you're a bright kid who truly wants to be somewhere in life and be someone, and we need that here at Townview. Congratulations."

All I could muster out at that point was, "Thank you."

I walked out and jumped in the air as soon as I made it to the parking lot outside.

I was so happy—running to the train station, yelling "Whoo!!!" and "YEAH!"

I was ecstatic for this moment because only an hour ago this feeling of excitement had been taken from me, and I had thought this dream was destroyed. God had other plans. As I was jumping for joy in the middle of the street, people kept passing by me thinking that I was out of my mind.

I was truly thankful for every teacher at Franklin MS who inspired me to keep climbing for the top and never settle for less. Around this time, I believed that everyone who had been a part of my life were there for a reason. Someone high above was definitely watching over me and had sent great people to restore a lost feeling inside of me that I thought was dead forever. I had to thank God, and I still do on a daily basis.

The whole train ride back to my house I kept thinking about how my friends at Franklin MS would react to the news about my new school. I had no other choice but to use my negotiation skills and tell them to all apply for Townview HS. Only six applied, two got in, and only one went with me—Jaziah. Jaziah was not part of the original group at Franklin, but still became one of my greatest friends. Omari had also been accepted into Townview, but he told me that he was moving to Hawaii to be with his uncle. So, we all knew that next year, it would only be me and Jaziah attending Townview. I was going to attend Townview Law Magnet and Jaziah would attend Townview Business Magnet.

I returned to my house with excitement and good news of be-ing accepted into Townview. As I walked in the front door, I saw my brother sitting on the couch and staring at another eviction notice in his hands. I immediately started to feel bad, knowing that my brother was stressed out. I felt terrible because I knew if I had a job, we would have extra money in the house and not have to stare at these eviction notices every other month. My brother looked beaten down. I knew that it was time for me to step up and make a big decision.

I sat down next to my brother and told him, "I'm dropping out after this year."

My brother lifted his head up and stared at me. He gave a stare that said, "That better not be the end of that statement."

I continued saying, "Bro, we need money in this house! If I drop out now, I can get a full time job so we can get some more money!"

My brother quickly countered back and said, "We need you to stay in school!"

My brother always treated me like an adult and let me make my own decisions, but he seemed so passionate about not letting me do this.

I had to fire something back, so I said, "But you dropped out, didn't you? Why can't I?"

My brother's face then saddened, and he had a look on his face of regret, shame, and embarrassment. He stood up, but proceeded to sit back down and pointed towards a seat for me to take as well.

He looked me in my eye with a very stern expression and said, "We've worked...you've worked way too hard to make it back to school, and I won't let you throw it away. I can't let that happen. Yeah, I dropped out, but I won't let you do the same. I'll make a deal with you. If I go back and get my GED, you have to promise me you'll go to Townview, graduate, and go on to college. Deal?"

I looked my brother in his eye and said, "Deal."

He then put out his hand for a handshake, but I gave him a hug instead. I loved making awkward moments for him. After agreeing to a deal with my brother, I continued with school.

The last day at Franklin MS had finally come, and we finished off the year by having a huge picnic at the school for all of the 8th graders. Everyone got their "end of the school year" fights in and said their final goodbyes to their fellow classmates that were going to different schools the next year. Our principal Mr. Jones, who everyone loved, declared he'd be going to Hillcrest as the new head principal. Everyone gave a warm Spartan cheer, which made that moment even more special. Nothing could've ruined that moment.

I returned home after school that day filled with exhaustion. I was glad to be home and looked forward to some much needed rest.

I made my way up the stairs to my door only to discover that the door had been locked with an eviction sign stuck to the front. The eviction notice my brother had been holding was finally enforced, and the reset button in my life had been pressed again. I just dropped down on the ground and thought to myself, "What's going to happen now?"

CHAPTER 7:

TIME TO BE A MAN

I was used to moving from place to place. In fact, I always had to move. By this time, I had attended seven different elementary schools, three different middle schools, and stayed in more than thirty different "homes." Even though change was a constant in my life, it never made the transitions any easier for me. I just felt numb. The feeling of change always took a toll on me.

I learned how to mask my feelings and avoid things that made me look back on what a true home looked like, but it was always hard to do. I would see Davis with his family and Omari with his family, and I'd nonetheless smile at what they had. You'd think that seeing their families together would make me sad, but in reality, it made me happy. It made me hopeful to know that true families still existed in the world.

Somewhere inside of me, I wanted this same feeling of a real family. I wanted to believe that one day I could have a real family of my own, but this aspiration was so buried in my head due to the lies, betrayals, and constant heartaches that I had experienced throughout my life. It made it very hard for me to believe that one day it could actually happen and be real for me. I was scared of achieving it but finding out in the end that it wasn't real.

I was happy to see families so tight, but I had accepted that this feeling of a "true family" and a "real home" was never going to be a part of my life. It would only remain a dream. Like my uncle said to me in the past, "It's time to face reality." I constantly repeated those words to myself. I accepted in my head that I would always have to move and people would always leave my life. I felt like nothing good was forever.

I thought to myself, "Wow, years later and my uncle's words still haunt me."

My uncle was harsh, but I couldn't stop making sense of his words. I knew it was time to grow up and be a man. I couldn't spend my time thinking of dreams and fairytales of a family, a home, and stuff that had been far away from me for a long time. I was 16 years old. Four years of my life had already flown by me. I had to grow up.

After I saw the eviction notice on the front door of our apartment, it knocked me from my dreamland back to my reality. I dropped down to my knees from mental exhaustion. I eventually managed to pick myself up, and I walked to a nearby train station. Justin picked me up from the train station about thirty minutes later, and he started briefing me about our new home in South Dallas.

Justin told me that it was a house and not an apartment this time. My brother always said he wanted a house where he could cut the grass and raise his kids, and now he felt like he had it. I was upset that our lives had been reset again and all of our property was locked inside of our former apartment, but I was happy to be moving out of North Dallas.

That neighborhood was always a problem for me. I had gotten punched in my face by a group of random guys looking for trouble. I had also been robbed by another group of random guys while bringing home groceries for my nieces to eat. I was just about fed up with that neighborhood, and I knew the next place that we were going to live had to be better.

When my brother picked me up, he said, "Hey, I found us a house and you're going to have your own room. It only costs $400 a month for a three bedroom. We now stay in South Dallas."

South Dallas? Our previous home was in the hood, but this new neighborhood was three times as worse. There's no wonder why he got the house at such a discount. I had pictured a house with a picket fence, nice green grass, and a big backyard.

When I arrived at the new house, it was an eye opener. The fence I had hoped for was definitely there, but the only problem was, it was alongside every window. Burglar bars, metal bars placed on the outside of the windows and doors to "prevent" a burglary, were mounted on each window and on both doors of the house.

They are added protection in more dangerous or poverty-stricken neighborhoods. It looked like we were staying in a prison.

In fact, every surrounding house had these burglary bars on them too. The local stores had metal bars on the doors, bulletproof glass separating the customer from the clerk, and a sign posted on the front of the store warning potential burglars/robbers that harm will be inflicted if they were to try anything "funny." The house had a big backyard, but it was overlooking an alleyway and gave a rear sideview of two liquor stores that had drug addicts constantly walking through them.

Drug addicts weren't uncommon for me to see. I could tell one from a mile away at this point. They were always in the alleyways. Either they were shooting up dope, trying to buy some drugs, or just so high that their minds were gone and they just wandered around like zombies. It also turned out that our house became available on the market because the previous occupants had the house raided by law enforcement personnel and were sent to prison for drug manufacturing and distribution.

In fact, our house was the only one on the block that *wasn't* a drug or gambling house. We would also have random drug addicts and sketchy guys come to our door from time to time looking for the previous occupants that had "helped" them in the past. Our neighbor's house even caught on fire and burned down to the ground when one addict tried to light something up inside of it. The police had briefed us on the whole incident when it happened.

Despite all of this negativity going on throughout my life, God kept my heart safe and my mind intact. He never let me forget the mission at hand, which was to not let the streets conform me and to make it out alive. God gave me something that took my mind off of troubles and kept hope alive inside. He gave me Townview Law Magnet. The school that was for brainiacs and kids that had the same ambitions as I did. We all wanted to make it far in life. In my mind, Townview was my way out of this place.

My freshman year at Townview was amazing. I didn't really know what to expect, but that all changed when the homework assignments started piling up in my backpack, along with tons of books. The teachers weren't lying when they said that this school was going to challenge us academically each day. I always prided myself on my work and did what I needed to do in order to get the grade I felt I deserved.

More importantly, the teachers were amazing. I made my move into the Criminal Justice section of Townview Law Magnet, and I quickly became one of their top students. There were students definitely blowing me out the water with their grades, but that doesn't necessarily make you a good student.

I was highly involved at the school. I participated in everything I could find within the Criminal Justice section of Townview.

Sophomore year I joined a program called Skills USA that allowed me to compete in law enforcement activities. At Townview, one of my sole missions was to develop more discipline. I had my brother in my life, but I felt like I needed more discipline and structure to be fully prepared for the future. I didn't want to be a reckless kid. I wanted to be a man of honor.

There wasn't a better place to be for this task than the JROTC program, which is the Junior Reserved Officer Training Corps program. I fell in love with JROTC and quickly rose through the ranks. Unlike some other schools that were just handing out ranks and promotions, we actually had to earn it at Townview. I wore my green pickle suit with pride, and I earned everything that was placed on that jacket. I wasn't handed anything, and it allowed me to be able to fight for something I wanted to have in life.

While at Townview, I made a friend named Hugo, who eventually became one of my best friends later on in life. Hugo was involved in the same activities that I was involved in at Townview, such as Skills USA and JROTC. We competed in everything together, and he also was a member of the Criminal Justice section of Townview. This made it even better for our friendship. We had two like minds. I made a great assortment of connections at Townview.

I even got a beautiful nerdy girlfriend who thought I was worth her time—Marcela Santos. Marcela claims it took me five hours to ask her out, but don't believe the hype. I was as smooth as a pile of rocks. Even though my clothes weren't stylish or new and my jokes certainly weren't getting any better, she always gave me her full attention and laughed at each joke I made. God please bless her heart. We both knew how awful those jokes were, but that didn't stop her from thinking they were the best. Marcela was my girl-friend and my best friend. She always helped me with whatever I needed, and her mom was always right there behind her to help out even more. She meant a lot to me, because she didn't see the clothes I wore or the fake smooth guy personality I tried to portray at times to impress her. Marcela just saw me, and that's honestly all I ever wanted out of anyone.

I had been judged, mocked, and teased countless times for the clothes I wore or the weird personality I possessed, but she, along with Omari, Kevin, Davis, Hugo, and all the other people I let in my life, only saw me for me and loved who "me" was inside. That's how I chose my friends and the people closest to me.

My teachers at Townview even showed that same love. Like the teachers at Benjamin Franklin Middle School, the teachers at Townview HS were always there to hear me out and help with any advice or assistance they were able to give. They were very im-pressed with the dedication and effort I would always give to the work I did at school. Everyone seemed to know the person I was when I was at school, but no one had a clue about my life at home or my journey everyday to school.

My march to school was definitely a journey. Townview was a Magnet school that received students from all over the school district. Their boundaries were the entire city of Dallas and not just one particular area of it. If a student wanted to take the school bus to Townview, they had to find the nearest high school by their house and that's where the Townview school buses would pick up the student. If they did not wish to take the school bus, then the student would have to find their own ride to school. This was a problem, because the nearest high school was about a mile and a half away from my house. That mile-and-a-half walk wasn't a normal stroll through the park or a suburban neighborhood. It was a journey through various street blocks where crime was very imminent.

The high school I had to walk to was Lincoln High School. It was not known for being very welcoming of new faces to the school. After arriving at Lincoln High School after school on the Townview bus, I almost lost my life on the journey back. Police officers were swarming the streets in front of Lincoln, breaking up fights, and trying to maintain order around the neighborhood. It was a chaotic scene that quickly spiraled out of control.

After that day, I knew that I could no longer return to that particular bus stop due to the high level of activity I had observed.

I knew that the public transit bus (DART) ran through the neighborhood, but I also knew that I didn't have a penny to get on the DART bus. After hours of thinking and consulting my internal reasoning, I decided to just walk to school.

Townview was about three miles away from my house. It consisted of a walk through numerous dangers, weather challenges, and a long bridge that had no way of escape except through the other side. I knew the potential dangers, so I had come up with a plan to leave the house at 6am every morning when everyone in the neighborhood was surely asleep. I knew the walk back would be bad since everyone in the neighborhood would be up at that time, but it was something I had to do.

We were required to wear our JROTC uniforms once a week. The crazy thing about it was that I had to walk from my house with the uniform on and try to keep it clean through every weather condition. It was either walk in it, or ball it up and shove it into my backpack. My commanding Sergeant, Sgt. Padilla, in JROTC, who was a former Texas Ranger and a Master Sergeant in the Army, never questioned me about my suit. When I made it to school sweaty, and my uniform shoes scuffed, Sgt. Padilla would just walk up to me and ask, "You alright Johnson?"

I would reply, "Yes sir."

And he would follow up with, "You're not lying to me, are you?"

And I would say, "No sir, I'm not."

He would just give me a stare as if he knew the exact struggles I endured everyday to get to school, but he didn't want to pressure me about it. He would tell me to go clean up before inspection, and as long as I did that, he was fine with it.

My cadet platoon sergeant, who was a student, tried to hassle me one day about my shoes and sweaty appearance, but Sgt. Padilla quickly cut him off and said, "Move to the next person."

Sgt. Padilla always had my back. He admitted to me a few years later that he knew I was going through tough times in my life, and he didn't want anyone to badger or scold me for going through something I had no control of at that time. He said that life was already hard enough on some people, and they didn't need others yelling at them for senseless things. Sgt. Padilla was always a good man.

I was a bit afraid of what could happen to me on the walks back and forth to school, but I was more afraid of losing out on an education like I did before. I didn't want to miss any more time from school, so I got up every morning at 6am, and walked to school through rain, sleet, and snow. I did it better than the local mailman. I walked three miles to school and another three miles back from school at the end of the day. The journey was about an hour and some change, but I would just pop in my headphones and drain the world out of my head.

I was chased by pit bulls, threatened numerous times while passing different groups all dressed in the same color, and I was even followed home on some occasions. It was dangerous, but I had no other choice. Every option to school was dangerous. I would see drug addicts (about fifty or sixty a day) walking around begging and searching for food, girls with cuts and bruises on their faces crying on the phone for the police to come, and groups of guys standing on their front porches daring me to look their way. I saw it all, but I only captured the image of going to school in my head.

Crossing the long bridge everyday was by far the worst of it all, because there was no way out. Once you were on the bridge there were only two options. You either had to walk all the way across it, or you had to turn around and go back through the entrance you came.

Public transit buses would pass me by every day. They would pass me about three times before I would even make it across the bridge. This went on for months and the buses never stopped, except for one day.

One day, I was wearing my JROTC uniform on my walk to school, and I had started to cross the "bridge of no return." A public transit DART bus started to pass me, as it did everyday, but this time it slowed down and stopped right next to me. The bus driver told me to get on, but I told him that I didn't have any money. He then repeated for me to get on, so I did. I tried telling him numerous times that I didn't have any money for the bus, but it was like talking to a wall.

He kept waving his hand as if to say, "Don't worry about it."

He talked over my words when I kept stating I didn't have any money.

He said, "What are you doing walking on this bridge boy? You are only a kid. Something could have happened to you!"

He spoke as though he was my long-lost and concerned father. He also spoke with a lot of passion, so I stayed quiet and continued to listen to him.

He then went on saying, "People have gotten kidnapped on this bridge and just the other day I read about kids getting kidnapped on a bridge in Houston. How long have you been walking this bridge?"

I told him, "For almost three months now,"

He shook his head back and forth saying, "No, no, no. That isn't right for a kid to have to do this. What school you go to?"

I said, "Townview."

And he said, "Townview? The smart school, right? I figured that's where you went. You don't seem like the normal kids in this neighborhood."

I kept looking out the front window because I had no clue where to get off.

He sensed my confusion and said, "Don't worry about it. I got you."

Another DART bus prepared to turn the corner in front of us, and the bus driver signaled to the other bus to hold on by honking a loud horn. The bus in front of us then came to a sudden halt.

The bus driver then looked at me and said, "You'll take that bus to the 8th and Corinth station, get off, and catch one of the three buses passing Townview high school."

I once again repeated to him for about the tenth time, "Sir, I don't have any money."

But once again, he repeated to me, "Don't worry about it." He then printed a one-day bus pass from his machine and said, "I don't ever want to see you on that bridge again. Ever. Stay in school, young man, and may God bless you."

I got off the bus and walked to the next bus with complete confusion. Tons of thoughts and questions went through my head: "Why would a total stranger help me? I had nothing to give yet he gave me something I greatly needed. Hundreds of buses had passed me up on that bridge every day, so why didn't he do the same? He could've kept going. Ms. Green could've gone about her day in the past and not concerned herself with my situation and let me go to Hillcrest. So why did she give her time and gas in her car to drive some kid to a school she wasn't even sure I'd commit to? Why did she even care? Pastor Wilson could've pretended like he didn't see me homeless on the streets and talked about me like everyone else did around him. Why did he make my problem his problem, and why did my cousin George make my problem his problem as well? My brother could've kept walking to his destination with my cousins that night I was choked and not have bothered to turn around and go back to my aunt's house. Why did he? What made him suddenly stop and turn around?"

These very questions haunted me the whole bus ride. It was almost like someone was watching over me. It was like someone was looking out for me and ensuring that I was safe and stayed on a certain path. A path where I didn't know where I was going, but something inside of me told me that I was supposed to be on it. It was no coincidence that I stumbled across these amazing people in my life, and it was no coincidence that I had walked across a bridge numerous times without being kidnapped or killed. It was almost like it was someone's plan for all of this to happen.

I knew at that very moment exactly who was looking out for me—God. He was always looking out for me.

Someone once told me, "Brion, you're a walking testimony. God must have something or someplace waiting for you that's going to be huge. Never forget that."

I knew then that God was keeping me safe, but what for? What did I have that was worth keeping me alive and safe? What did I ever do? I knew God was taking me somewhere, but where? I'm a poor kid who has always struggled and lived in poverty, so why me? I have nothing to offer anyone. Why help me stay alive? Thoughts continued to cross inside of my head, and I started to feel really sick in my stomach. I was saved from my swarm of thoughts when the bus had come to a stop, and the bus driver informed everyone that we were now at 8th and Corinth Station.

I quickly tried to pull myself together and clear those thoughts by saying, "No, I'm a poor kid who has always been poor and alone, and that's exactly how it has to be. There's no other place for me than right here, and there's no other plan besides the one I have right now. The bus driver's act and the acts in the pasts were just coincidences."

I tried to get myself to believe this, but I never could. I just didn't want to believe that there was so much hope for me. I didn't want to be crushed like all the other times in my life. I had a funny feeling that the bus driver's act wouldn't be the last of these "coincidences." I was scared for what God's plan was for my life. It was a plan that consisted of much more than just a simple kid in poverty. I had a plan to keep my life the way it was, but God had a different plan in mind. I just didn't know what it was at that time.

* * *

When I finally made it to school, I was led to tell some of the administrators about my difficult journeys to school everyday and the harsh life I had. Townview supplied me with a pack of free DART bus tickets through a program in school. The program was for kids living in poverty that couldn't afford to pay for bus tickets on a daily basis. From that day on, I started catching the public DART bus to school.

It seemed with every positive step forward, a negative wasn't too far behind. The house I lived in was rough, and the neighborhood I lived in was worse. When I returned back to my own house, reality would hit harder than any punch ever thrown at me.

Our house was a rundown place that always had something not working in it. Our landlord never fixed anything. He would come by at the first of the month to collect rent, but that was the only time we ever saw him. One day the air conditioning (AC) stopped working and my nieces were profusely sweating in the house because of it. In the Texas heat, you won't make it far without AC in your home. Even though the AC was broken and we had asked the landlord several times to fix it, he never did. The landlord didn't care about making an effort to fix the AC until the day I told my school administrators at Townview Law Magnet about the situation.

They made it quite clear to the landlord that he'd have a big legal battle on his hands if changes weren't expeditiously made in our home. After hearing from my school administrators, the landlord quickly sprinted to our home that day and fixed everything we'd been asking him to fix.

The landlord then came to me and asked, "We're good right? You gonna let your people know I fixed everything?"

I said, "Yeah we're good, for now."

It felt good to know I had people watching my back, but more importantly, we had our AC.

Everything felt like it was finally coming back together for everyone in the house. Time was now passing by, and it looked as though we had crossed into the Golden Age of peace in our lives. This was the perception, but like I said earlier, with every good thing that came along in my life, trouble was somewhere near. I came home from school one day and saw my brother sitting on the porch.

By this time, Justin had gone back to school and gotten his GED, and I was extremely proud of him for keeping his promise to me. He looked stressed out on the porch, and this scene had looked all too familiar. He had the same face my mother had when I had come home from Oakville Middle School the day she left us. I started to feel sick as if something bad was about to happen.

I approached him and asked, "What's up with you?"

He then lifted up his head, stared at me and said, "I'm leaving. I'm going back to St. Louis."

I couldn't believe what I had just heard. He started giving me reasons that led to his decision like relationship problems, money problems and limited opportunities for him to succeed in Texas. While he was explaining his reasons for the move, I couldn't help but reminisce about the moment when my mom had told us that she was leaving. I couldn't believe my ears. I was sure that someone was playing a trick on me, but this was reality at its finest. Here he was, the man who had taken care of me since he was 17, saying that he was leaving. I can't even recollect my emotions at that point, but I was deeply hurt.

My brother proceeded to say, "You can either choose to go with me back to St. Louis or see if Ma will take you in New Jersey."

My brother looked really sad as if he had just noticed that he was essentially doing the same thing our mother had done years ago.

Suddenly, emotions swept away from me, and I stood up straight and said, "I choose neither. I'm staying in Texas."

I wish I could show my brother's facial expression at this point, because his face said more than a million words. I uttered those words and took a firm stance. I had been running around everywhere with my brother for years from house to house, place to place, but not this time. I was tired of it. I was tired of going where people told me to go, and I decided at that point, I would take control of my own life. I was tired of having the reset button pressed on my life, and Texas was the only place I felt I needed to be.

I knew that if I stayed in Texas, I had a chance to make it. I knew that if I returned to St. Louis, hope would be lost forever. I wanted to make decisions for myself now. To me, that was my transition to becoming a man. My brother had always taught me that a man is someone who owns up to his responsibilities. Someone who makes decisions for his own life and accepts the consequences that come with those decisions. I learned those lessons, and I was ready to take control of my own life. I made my decision, and I was prepared to face all consequences that came with it.

I was expecting my brother to yell or get mad, but he didn't.

He simply looked at me and said, "Alright. I've always treated you like a man and now you've just made a man's decision. I respect that. The landlord said that he's evicting us in two weeks. You have two weeks to find a place to stay."

When my brother uttered those words, the hunt began.

Texas was the first and only place that ever made me feel like I belonged. I thought it was only in movie films where you got a feeling inside that tells you "This is where I'm supposed to be," but I had received it with full force. Here was another situation where my dreams could get stripped away again, but this time, I wasn't having it. I wasn't going to sit back and return to the very place I knew wanted to destroy me. I wasn't going to return, and I meant that.

I searched high and low for a place to stay, but none of these places seemed right to me. Time was ticking, and with each day that passed, stress was at an all-time peak in my head. I was so full of stress and tension that the people closest to me got the worse of the backlash.

I knew I was headed for a crash-course landing if I didn't get my head straight. It was a hard task to do since I had nowhere to live and eviction was now in two days. Things were not looking pretty for me. That night, I made it back to the house slumped and very depressed.

My brother came into my room and told me, "Hey, I just talked to Ma and she's sending money for me to catch the bus back to St. Louis. I'm leaving tomorrow morning." He then asked, "So, have you found a place?"

I told him, "No."

And he said, "Well, there's only two days left."

I told him, "I know," and he told me to keep trying.

I felt like my dream in Texas had finally reached its end.

I sat down in my room and thought to myself, "Man, I could really use one of those 'coincidences' in my life to happen right about now."

I felt like if I was truly supposed to be in Texas and that gut feeling I had wasn't just stomach acid, then something out of the ordinary would have to happen right now to keep me in Texas. I then closed my eyes and tried to sleep for the night.

The ringing of my cellphone woke me up in the middle of the night. It was a number I had not seen before, so I answered with caution.

The voice on the other end responded to my "hello" by saying, "Hey baby, it's your Aunt Pam. Your grandma's sister. I live here in Dallas, and I heard you needed a place to stay?"

I quickly responded, "Yes ma'am," and she told me that I could move in first thing on Saturday morning, which was the day after tomorrow. I said "thank you" over a thousand times and then hung up the phone.

I could not believe what had just happened. Turns out my brother had put in a call to my great aunt a long while back, and she was just now returning the call. Talk about clutch timing. These "coincidences" were starting to get a bit out of control, but little did I know, they had only just begun. God had my number, and he was not finished using it.

CHAPTER 8:

AN UNEXPECTED TURN

I was 18 years old and had officially moved in with my Aunt Pam in Pleasant Grove, a neighborhood in southeast Dallas. Living with my aunt felt different, because I didn't have my brother by my side. My brother had officially left the state of Texas and moved back to St. Louis. I greatly missed my brother and was sad that he left, but I knew it was time for me to start my own life in Texas. Living with my aunt created a stable and simple life for me. It wasn't a lavish lifestyle and it wasn't in the best neighborhood, but our street was pretty quiet for the most part. I had my own room, cable, my own videogame system and a guard dog in the house. I didn't know much more a teenage boy could ask for in his life. I had a peaceful home and a good school to attend. I was still going to school at Townview, making pretty good grades, and I even joined the Dallas Police Explorers program in my neighborhood.

The Dallas Police Explorers program was a way for teenagers to get acquainted with the job/role of a police officer. I signed up for the Explorers program, because my teachers at Townview recommended it to me. I had tremendous respect for my teachers at

Townview who were former police officers, judges, and family violence advocates. Those teachers gave me a new outlook on law enforcement and the criminal justice career field as a whole. They convinced me to go to an Explorer's meeting.

I initially had mixed feelings about joining the program, due to my past experiences with police officers, but I still decided to do it. I wanted to believe that more people like my teachers at Townview existed in the world. I decided to at least give it a chance, and I was happy that I did. The police officers that ran the Explorers program were great cops and taught me a lot about law enforcement. They had my back on several occasions and changed my outlook about police officers.

I was walking home from a Dallas Police Explorers meeting one day, and four guys tried to rob me for my Beats headphones that Davis's family had bought me. They circled around me and demanded that I give them my headphones or they'd beat me up. I refused. I just continued walking, and they became more aggressive with me. One of the guys started to approach me with his fist balled up as if he was going to hit me.

Just then, a Dallas Police squad car pulled up next to us. The car doors opened and out stepped two of the police officers from the Police Explorers program. They asked if there was a problem, and the four guys stated "no" and that we were all just playing around. The officers sensed the tension and knew it was a lie. They asked the four guys to say my first and last name, and the four guys just looked around in the sky and at the ground. The officers then told me that I needed better "friends" and told me that they would give me a ride home.

I never forgot how great it felt to have people in my corner who stood against bullies. They were brave, kind, and I respected them for it. They were different than the officers in my past, and they showed me good examples of how officers should be. I was happy that good cops came into my life and gave me a new perspective about police officers. I was also grateful that they had just saved me from a potential robbery. They also gave me a vision for my future: I saw myself protecting others like those officers had protected me. I started to envision myself in their position.

* * *

I was sure that God had placed me in my Aunt Pam's house so that I could stay there for a long time, but God had bigger plans for my life. I still attended church at Lovers Lane and attended the youth group. The Youth Ministry was in the process of welcoming in a new youth pastor. The church decided to welcome in the new youth pastor with a pool party in the home of a family that attended the church. In all honesty, I wanted to go, but I had many challenges that prevented that for me.

My church was in north Dallas, and I lived in southeast Dallas. I had to take the public transportation system, DART, and it was like a two-to-three hour journey to the pool party from where I lived. The party started around 5pm, which meant that I would have to take the DART back home after dark. The last time I had taken the DART by myself at night, a group of people wearing black masks robbed everyone on the train. I was definitely not going to put myself in that position again. I would also have to stand in the Texas heat and wait for the DART bus. The DART bus in my neighborhood was either running behind schedule or way ahead of schedule but never on time. I had every reason not to go to that party, so why couldn't I stop thinking about going?

I was laying in my bed, and I had just turned on my Playstation for a nice relaxing Sunday with videogames. I had my snacks ready for the day, and I was comfortable in my bed. Yet another feeling came across me. It was an uneasy and restless feeling in my gut. Something inside of me said, "You need to go to that pool party tonight." I didn't know it at the time, but that voice/feeling inside of me was about to lead me to a better life. It's weird writing this and thinking about what life I would've had if I never went to that party, but I'll save the reveal. When that voice inside of me told me to get up and go, I did it without a moment of hesitation. I grabbed my backpack, put my drinks and snacks in the bag, and went to the bus stop.

I had to catch a bus to a train, then switch trains, then take another bus, then walk from the bus stop to the house. It took me over three hours to reach north Dallas, but the closer I got, the more the uneasy feeling started to lighten up as if it was telling me "You're on the right path."

I approached the house of the pool party, and it was huge with a gate that surrounded it. I remember feeling like the *Fresh Prince of Bel Air* while I was approaching this large house, which I considered to be a mansion. Even though it was a big house, I was not easily fascinated by the extravagant lifestyle. I remember thinking to myself that it was a nice house for the owners of the home, but I had my own path to worry about in life. I couldn't get caught up in my imagination.

There was a note posted on the front door of the home, advising all guests to go to the backyard. After reaching the backyard, I felt more at ease seeing familiar faces and a lot of my friends from church at the party. While I was catching up with a few friends, a woman at the pool party kept approaching me and asking me if I wanted something to eat or drink. Each time she asked me, I respectfully declined with a "no ma'am."

She must've approached me about seven or eight times during the party. At this point in my life, I learned not to take things from people or create any kind of hassle. I always sat back and tried to be the least amount of "needy" as possible.

I walked by my pastor, Grant, who was talking to a group of people like he always did, but this time, I heard him say my name. When I walked past him, he stopped talking and greeted me. I knew Grant was a good guy and I had enough trust in him that he wasn't saying anything bad about me, but I didn't want to be the center of his discussion with the group.

I looked at the sky and saw that the sun had started to set for the day. I still had enough time on the clock to make it close to my house before the sun completely went down and before the trains became a dangerous adventure. A friend at the party, Ruby, had agreed to take me to a nearby train station. The party started to clear out and only a few guests were remaining at the house.

The group that Pastor Grant was talking to at the party had also started a conversation with me. The group started asking many questions about my life, and I soon discovered that all of the guests at the party had already left. The people that were questioning me about my life were the owners of the home with their family.

I remember checking the time, thinking to myself, "I really have to go before it gets late," but I was a different type of kid.

Even though it was getting late, respect was more important to me. I saw it as disrespectful to leave midway in the conversation, so I stayed. I also enjoyed just sitting down and talking to them. They seemed like nice people.

Ruby advised me that she would be heading out, and I told her that she could leave without me. I stayed and talked more with the owners of the home, Walter and Angela Wilson. Walter's sister and her husband were also there, Trevor and Debra. Walter and Angela's 5-year-old daughter, Lucy, then approached me and asked if I wanted some food, and I respectfully declined.

Then Lucy said, "But if you don't eat, you won't grow."

I laughed and agreed to eat some pizza.

The night sky had fully taken its position, and the shade outside had turned into shadows. I looked over at the clock and saw that it was nearly my curfew to be home. I told the family that I should be heading home now, and Angela stated that she understood. She then looked over at Walter with big eyes, and Walter looked confused by the message she was trying to send to him. Angela nodded at him and then nodded her head in my direction.

Walter finally caught on and said, "Brion, can I give you a ride home?"

I gave Walter the directions to my home, and we were on our way to Pleasant Grove.

Walter had a really nice car. It was a black Lexus, and I had never been in one before. I remember the entire car ride thinking about his safety in my neighborhood. The combination of his appearance with the nice black Lexus he was driving was not a good recipe in Pleasant Grove. A recipe like that would only lead to trouble and a potential robbery. Luckily, Walter's black Lexus had a dark enough tint on it to not be able to see inside of the car.

When we arrived at my house, I got out of the car and said, "Thank you."

When I walked into the house that night, I honestly thought to myself that it would be my last time ever seeing Walter and Angela, but I was wrong.

My mother had finally managed to scrape up enough money together and booked me a round trip plane ticket to Newark, New Jersey to see her. There was only one problem; I didn't have enough money to travel from Pleasant Grove all the way to the airport. My aunt was working throughout the day, so she couldn't take me. I didn't even know where the airport was located at the time, and as far as I knew, the public transit didn't go directly to the airport.

I only had $40 in my pocket, and I knew that it wouldn't be enough money to catch a cab to the airport. This was before Uber and Lyft ever existed, so options were limited. It was either the train, bus or a cab if you didn't have access to a car. I came up with a plan that I would travel as far north as possible on the DART train and try to catch a cab to the airport from there.

I made it to the train, and I started finding flaws in my plan. I started thinking, "What if I am actually further away from the airport when I travel north? How will I pay the driver if the fare is more than $40? I won't have any money for food or transportation from the Newark airport if I use it all now."

My plan was quickly falling apart. I was behind schedule and rapidly losing time. I started to lose faith, but God gave me a blessing. It was like my guardian angel heard my pain and my doubts. I received a random text from Walter, asking how I was doing in life. Angela texted me right after that and asked a similar question. I remember thinking, "How did they get my number?" and "Why did they decide to text me?"

I texted Angela and told her that I was heading northbound on the DART train to the airport. Angela told me that she was currently in the downtown area running errands with her younger sister, Brenda. She asked me what train station I was currently at, and I told her that the train was about to stop at the Pearl Station, which is also in the downtown area. (Side note: I'm a strong believer that there are no coincidences and that everything happens for a reason.) Angela quickly found the location of the Pearl train Station and told me to get off at that stop. She told me that the place she was with her sister was only a few blocks from the Pearl Station. Talk about a strong blessing that's right on time. I got off of the train, and within a few minutes, I was in the car with Angela and Brenda, two people who I barely knew but were willing to help me.

Being a teenager who had never owned a car, I seriously underestimated the speed of a car. I was honestly amazed at how much time you could save by driving a vehicle. We were up north so fast that we actually flipped the hands of time, and I was now way ahead of schedule. We even had time to pick up something to eat.

Angela was always concerned about me eating food. I was a very scrawny kid. I didn't really notice it, but throughout all of my trials in life, my body suffered a lot. Every time I looked in the mirror and saw myself, I reflected on the life I had undergone so far. I thought about the many meals I missed out on, the meals I snuck and was punished for, and the people closest to me who were eating while I starved. Those memories always crushed me the most. My mother always taught me that the "free things" in life are often times more expensive in the end, so I didn't take things from people when they were offered to me. I always kept that in mind. Angela meant no harm by offering me food, but the defenses in my head were always triggered. It was like PTSD crept into my head.

We finally arrived at the airport, and Angela made me promise her that I'd eat something inside. I never broke a promise. She then gave me a hug and told me to have a safe flight. When she hugged me, I felt her put something inside of my pants pocket. I didn't check it until I received my plane ticket inside of the airport, and I saw that it was cash that she had put into my pocket. I don't remember the exact amount, but it was at least $100. I was lost for words. Here I was, earlier in the day worrying about how I was going to make it to the airport on time and how I was going to stretch

$40, and now I had more than $100. I didn't know exactly how I felt about it, but I accepted it nonetheless. I took it as a blessing.

When I made it to New Jersey, I was happy to see my mother. No matter what she had done in the past, I could never get the love I had for her to fade away. It was always there, and I enjoyed being with her. I felt secure in our connection each time I visited her, even though I knew it was only going to be short lived. I always tried to enjoy each moment with her that I could.

While I was in New Jersey, Angela texted me asking about my trip and what I had been doing while in New Jersey. There was a commercial on television for the new Derrick Rose 9.8 shoes that were just released, and I told her about it. The very next day, there was a knock at the door. The man on the other side stated that he was with UPS and that he had a package for me. I didn't order anything and neither did my mom, so I refused to open the door. Then the UPS worker became more impatient and told me that he was leaving if I didn't take the package. He then dropped the box on the ground and left down the hallway.

I slowly opened the door and quickly took the UPS package on the ground. The package was addressed to me. I opened it up, and there were the Derrick Rose 9.8 shoes from the commercial. I couldn't even imagine being able to afford a pair, and now I had them. I didn't even ask for them.

I remember having mixed feelings. A part of me wanted to be excited because I now had the shoes, but the other part of me questioned her kindness. I couldn't think of any reason why she would want to help a kid like me, who had nothing to offer back. I didn't know how to feel. Angela continued to send more gifts afterwards without my knowledge. I started to feel uneasy about the situation, so I contacted my friends and family for advice, but it only created more confusion about the whole situation. I received a bunch of mixed responses from everyone I spoke with throughout the week.

Some people were all for Angela and Walter being in my life. They argued that I should be grateful for the gifts the Wilson family bought me and keep them. They even suggested that I start making special requests for her to buy me more extravagant things. They essentially wanted me to use her, stating that her money would be beneficial to me. But that's not who I am. I will never be that person. Ever. I never wanted to be a charity case or have things just given to me. I was definitely not a person to ever use someone else.

Some of my other friends and family argued a different point. They argued that the Wilson family was bad for my life and that Angela and Walter were the ones using me to make themselves look better. They stated that Angela could be using me to show everyone how "good" she was by helping a troubled kid, and she could be trying to have her own "Blindside story," like the movie.

All of the feedback I had received made my head hurt. I was just an 18-year-old teenager at this time and had no idea what to do. I knew that I had to make up my mind about the family, or I'd be lost in my head forever. My mother always taught me that if I wanted to know the truth about someone then I would need to go directly to the source. I called Angela and told her that we needed to talk.

I remember speaking very sternly to Angela about not wanting to receive any more gifts and not wanting any more help from her. I told her that she was a good person, but I didn't want anything else from her. Angela explained her side of not meaning to cause any harm, and she stated that she just felt it inside of herself to help me. Angela really did have good intentions, but I wasn't willing to take the risk of being used again in life. I had already been a victim too many times, and I wasn't going to let it happen again. At the end of the conversation, Angela agreed to respect my wishes and not gift anything else to me.

Even though I had argued my point and had received the response I wanted, I felt bad. I felt like I may have spoken too harshly to someone who could've legitimately been helping without expecting something in return. Because I started feeling badly about everything, I called my grandmother.

By this time, my grandmother and I had reconciled, and like I said about my mother, I couldn't forget the love she gave me. Love is so much stronger to me than holding hate towards anyone. I called my grandmother and explained everything to her. She told me that I let too many people enter into my head and that too many voices inside of my head would cause me to lose my own voice.

She told me that I needed to look inside of myself and figure out what Cortez wanted and how Cortez felt. (My grandmother always called me by my middle name "Cortez" and never Brion.) I told her that if I trusted the Wilson family, I could be setting myself up to get hurt again. I didn't have much energy left inside of me to get broken down in life.

My grandmother told me, "Yes, that could be possible. They could be bad for your life. But look at it this way, what if you're refusing a blessing from God? You could be denying the very blessing he intended for your life. These people could be your next path in life that God has sent for you."

That hit me more than anything I had heard from anyone else! My grandmother always had the best advice and was a very wise woman. She was never rich or wealthy, but she had so much more experience in life that she had gained and understood. Her words entered directly into my heart, and that gut feeling came back. My voice had come back, and I now understood what " Cortez wanted." It was like everything inside of me had agreed with her at one time. It felt right. I then contacted Angela to speak with her again.

Angela told me that she and Walter were in New York City for Walter's business conference and that she wanted to meet with me in New York since I was staying in New Jersey. I agreed to meet her in New York, and I took the public transit into Manhattan. I had been to New York City in the past with my mom, but this trip to New York was different.

I met up with Angela, and we toured Central Park in a bike carriage ride. We then went to a restaurant, and she attempted to get me to order food, but once again, the past started to seep into my head. I started to question her motives again. I didn't want her paying for anything. I just kept telling her that I wasn't hungry.

Angela called my mother and asked her what she could do to get me to order food and eat. My mother advised Angela to give me time and to back off a bit, but Angela's passion to help me was too great to listen at the time. Angela handed me the phone, and I spoke with my mom. Angela got up and walked outside of the restaurant. I felt bad at this point, because I naturally cared for others. I felt bad that I was making her feel bad—if that makes sense.

I walked outside of the restaurant, approached Angela, and said, "I'm sorry."

I never wanted anyone to feel bad because of me.

Angela told me, "No, it's not you. I'm not upset with you. It just hurts knowing that someone hurt you so bad in your life that you're not even willing to take help from people now."

As soon as she said those words, I just felt tears falling from my eyes. She was right. I was hurt so many times in my life that I felt like I couldn't trust anyone. Life wasn't fair for me, but I felt like I wasn't fair with Angela. It wasn't fair that she had to pay for the costs of what others had done to me in my past.

At that moment, I went against my own PTSD, defense mechanisms, and past pain to open the doors again to trust. I realized that I had closed the doors to trust in my head to block bad people from entering into my life, but when I did that, I also blocked out a lot of good people from being able to enter my life. I knew everyone walking by us thought that Angela and I were crazy for crying together in the middle of a mall, but we didn't care.

I looked at Angela and told her, "I promise you that I will try. I will try."

I meant "trying" in the sense of being able to trust again. I meant those words. I couldn't guarantee perfection, but I could genuinely "try." Angela said that my "trying" was perfect for her. I had no idea at the time, but Angela and Walter were about to change my life, and this time, it was going to be changed in a positive way.

Angela told me that our next destination was the Nike shop. I had never been to the Nike shop before. Each floor of the Nike store was a different sport. Anyone who knows me knows that basketball is my passion. I was in love with basketball. Heck, it was basketball that led me to make a lot of friends in Texas.

We went to the basketball floor of the Nike store, and Angela said that she was going to get coffee. Angela told me that I could walk around with the store attendant and that I could get whatever I wanted. I found out years later that Angela left to get coffee because she thought that I'd feel more comfortable choosing items if she wasn't hovering over me. Anyone else in my position would have gone crazy and got everything they wanted, but of course, me being me, I stayed modest.

I was still a bit uncomfortable with everything. I remember checking the price tags on the items I saw in the store, and I put it right back down after seeing how much it cost. I finally managed to get a pair of basketball shorts and some socks that were reasonably priced.

Then the attendant who was walking with me asked, "Who was that white lady that was with you? Is this some type of charity program you're in?"

When I heard that, I was mad.

I simply responded, "No."

My body tensed up more, and I put the two items I had chosen right back on the store shelves. Those were the thoughts I knew people would have about everything going forward with Angela, and my pride was too much for me to be seen that way.

When Angela came back from getting her coffee, she asked, "Where's the stuff you got?"

Angela was confused to see nothing in my hands.

She asked the store attendant, "What happened? I thought you were going to help him choose items."

The store attendant quickly responded, "Don't worry, I saw everything he was looking at!"

Angela and the sales attendant went around the store, picking everything from the store shelves. They were consulting amongst themselves on which items I would need and which items I would like the most. Since I was still in my feelings about the store attendant's comment, I wasn't being much help to them with choosing the items. They pretended I wasn't there and chose everything themselves.

Angela turned towards me and told me to choose a pair of shoes. In my head, I was still in my feelings, so I said that I didn't want any shoes. Then I looked up at the shoe rack and saw the perfect pair of shoes—a pair of gray Nike LeBron 8 lows. Everyone in my circle knows that I am one of the biggest LeBron James fan club members alive. LeBron had barely started creating shoes at the time, but his shoes were really expensive. They were about $300. That may not seem like a lot of money to some people, but for a kid like me from the hood, who lived in a rough area, $300 was a fortune for shoes. I thought I would never own a pair of Lebron James shoes in my life, and here they were waiting for me to choose them.

I picked up the LeBron shoes, and they were perfect. I was a little embarrassed in the store, because the shoes that I already had on were really worn out and looked beat down. I also didn't choose the best socks to wear that day, so I was hesitant to take off my shoes and try on the Lebron James shoes. Despite my embarrassment, I decided to try on the Nike Elite socks with the Lebron shoes.

When I first put on the shoes with the socks, everything felt so comfortable. I finally had good shoes with good soles in them. It felt like I was walking on pillows when I took my first steps in the shoes. I had developed plantar fasciitis from my old shoes, but that was soon resolved with the combination of the padded socks and the comfy Lebron shoes.

I was super nervous leaving the store wearing the shoes, because I didn't want the attendants to think that I was stealing from the store. Angela assured me that I could do it, and the sales attendant also stated that it was okay. When we were at the cash register, I looked at the running total for the items Angela was buying for me, and it said "$1,000." The attendant was still ringing up additional items. Angela noticed that I was looking at the price, becoming more disheartened about someone spending that much money on me, so she quickly turned the price screen so I couldn't see it. After buying out the Nike store, we returned to the business district.

After touring the city for the day, I decided to stay in New York at the hotel with Angela and Walter. The hotel staff was able to bring in a nice bed for me to sleep on in the living room. That night, I remember looking outside at the city through the hotel window. Everything felt like a dream. I was more accepting of the moment, because I didn't feel like it was real. I felt like the next day, I would wake up and everything would've been a dream. But it wasn't.

This was real, and it was happening to my life. I even started to feel a little sick to my stomach when I tried to put a grasp on reality. I felt like Neo in the *Matrix* when he was first taken out of the matrix and brought into a new reality. My stomach turned when I tried to understand everything, so I accepted it as a dream and I was content with it. I didn't know what my future held or where my new path would take me, but I knew everything would soon change.

* * *

When I say everything was going to change, everything changed! When I returned to Texas, Angela and Walter asked me to move in with them. I initially declined, because I was content with the life that I already had in Pleasant Grove with my Aunt Pam. Yeah, my life wasn't flashy or perfect, but I was happy with it.

At my Aunt Pam's house I had my own room, food when I wanted it, a loving aunt who cared, and I attended the number one school in the nation. In my head, everything was already set in a good way for my life. To move in with Angela and Walter would mean that I had to be willing to risk stability for uncertainty, and it was too high of a risk for me to take.

My pastor, Grant, pulled me aside in church and said, "Listen, this family's going to ask you to move in with them again. I'm going to need you to say yes this time. You've been through a lot. Take blessings as they come to you."

After speaking with my pastor, I had a long talk with my Aunt Pam that night. We talked about some of my fears with the possible change of living with the Wilson Family. Aunt Pam reassured me that if at any point I felt uncomfortable or regretted the move with the Wilson family, my room was always open at her house. With Aunt Pam's reassurance, I felt more comfortable with my decision. I spoke with Angela and Walter and agreed to move in with them.

Soon after, the Wilson family paid for me to attend a church retreat, The Boys to Men Retreat. My youth ministry group was traveling to Colorado and camping out in the wilderness. Pastor Grant said that we would also hike two mountains, including Long Peaks Mountain, which is a 14,259 foot mountain.

A lot of people doubted me on that trip, because they thought that a guy like me wouldn't be able to make it to the top. I was a city boy from a rough neighborhood, and I had never even been close to a mountain. The journey to the top of that mountain was difficult, and I had no hiking experience. I may not have hiked a mountain before, but this wasn't my first time dealing with adversity and doubts. I took everything life had put me through to hike this mountain.

This wasn't my first time being ice cold, this wasn't my first time feeling pain, and this wasn't the first time I had to keep pushing through challenges. I wasn't raised a quitter. I was raised a mental fighter. I knew that if I quit, the mental pain would be a lot worse than the pain I was already feeling. So, I pushed through it.

While hiking up the mountain, I encountered multiple challenges with the cold weather, physical exhaustion, altitude sickness, and near-death experiences (almost slipping off the mountain a few times). Despite every adversity I faced on that hike, I made it to the top. When I reached the top of the mountain and looked around, I saw everyone with big shocked eyes looking at me. Astonished.

I immediately dropped down to my knees and held my arms up in the air with my fists tightly clinched. I made it. I was proud of what I had just accomplished and couldn't believe that I was on top of an actual mountain. I never thought in a million years that I would reach the top of a mountain, but here I was with my arms in the air taking in every second of the moment.

The leader of the hiking trip, Jeff, walked over to me and said, "I'm not going to lie. I didn't think you would make it. But when I saw you reach the top of the mountain, I said to myself that this kid is special. There's something in him. You've got heart."

I took it for what it meant. I had been a fighter my whole life. I always felt that I had no other choice in life. I felt like I had to fight in life or I would lose everything in me. And now, people were starting to see that fighting spirit in me.

I took one last look from the top of the mountain. Words cannot truly describe the view. Everything seemed as though it was constructed into one great masterpiece. The hills, the mountains, and the snow sprinkled on everything created a memory that stuck in my head forever. I thanked God for my journey to the top, and took the hiking experience as a valuable lesson in life.

When I returned back to the Wilson house from the retreat, the Wilson family sat me down to talk about the possibility of changing schools. They wanted me to change from Townview and go to a small private school called Dallas Lutheran. I was completely against the idea. I was happy being at Townview with all of my friends. Even though I was against the idea, I had agreed to at least go to Dallas Lutheran for a meeting with the Principal.

Principal Nitz showed me a very brief tour of the small Lutheran school since it only consisted of about three hallways. After the tour, we returned to his office and started speaking about what Lutheran had to offer me as a student, but I was barely listening to him since my mind was already set on Townview. I stood up and told him that I appreciated the offer, but I was not interested in the school.

Mr. Nitz stood up and told me, "What if I could give you a year of your life back?"

With those words, he caught my attention. I looked at him with eyes that were fully attentive for his next words.

He continued, "I see that you already have a good portion of your core classes completed, and we could double down on some of the core classes that you're missing. Doing those things would mean that you could graduate as a Senior this year."

I was an incoming Junior and had lost two years of my school life due to the hardships in my past, but now Mr. Nitz was offering me a year of my school life back. I desperately wanted to be back in the correct grade level that I was supposed to be. This was my chance to at least get one step closer to it. Mr. Nitz had my full attention.

He went on, "It won't be easy. It'll take a lot of effort on your part, but we can make it happen. Your family told me a little of your journey in life. I know if anyone can do this, it's you. What do you say?"

Mr. Nitz extended his hand towards me. I thought about everything I have been through so far, and I knew what I had to do. I looked back at him, and I shook his hand. I told him that I'd be honored to attend his school.

I don't think I truly knew what I had signed up for, but then again, when does anyone exactly know what's going to happen in the future? I knew it wouldn't be easy, but I was ready. Life had taken an unexpected turn for me in such a short period of time, but it wasn't the first time life had thrown a twist my way. I was ready for God's plan for my life. I felt that God was changing my life for the better. God's plan was still unknown to me, but I knew I would be in a better place when it was all said and done.

CHAPTER 9:

A NEW WAY OF LIFE

I had just moved in with the Wilson Family in a neighborhood known as Preston Hollow, which is located in north Dallas. The neighborhood was wealthy, the buildings looked to be in mint condition and luxury vehicles swarmed the area. I felt out of place. Everything seemed like it was happening so quickly. I went from Pleasant Grove to Preston Hollow in a blink of an eye. Based on the area alone, I knew that living with the Wilson family would be different from any life I had ever known.

The Wilson household included Walter and Angela, Angela's younger sister Brenda, Lucy (5), Grayson (3) and Owen (3). Brenda was, I believe, 16 at the time, and Angela had full custody of her. I had met Brenda in my youth group, so we weren't complete strangers. Together, we all accepted the new change since it wasn't just a change for me. The kids initially had a blank stare like, "Who is this new guy in our house?" But after a few hours, they accepted the "new guy" and welcomed me as a new addition to the family.

I brought all of my belonging in suitcases and balled up blankets. I initially refused to unpack, because I didn't want to get too comfortable. I figured that my new life at their home wouldn't last long before the "reset button" was pressed, and I'd be forced to leave. Constant change was always a part of my life. I had many doubts in my head about the new transition, but the Wilson family tried their best to make my transition into their home a special one.

Angela went out of her way to decorate my room with posters of Lebron James, my celebrity crushes, and my favorite music artists. Angela also hung up a huge picture that was taken of me when I had made it to the top of the mountain. I was shocked that Angela had managed to decorate the room as if it was made just for me. I never had a stable home to put personalized things on the wall or change my room's appearance. Walter also went out of his way to equip me with a laptop and a desk area in my room, which was needed for the upcoming school year. They even replaced my entire wardrobe with new clothes. It was their way of telling me that I wouldn't be leaving anytime soon and that this room was mine.

Everything was so new to me. The Wilson family had people who would come to the house and clean the rooms on a daily basis. We had family dinners together and even asked about each others' days. This was a huge change for me since I mostly kept to myself. We even had a day when we went out and took family pictures together.

For my 19th birthday, the Wilson family took me to a nice restaurant called Javiers. This was an important moment for me in my life, because I really only celebrated my birthday maybe twice in my lifetime. My mother worked so much in the past, but she never had the money to do much for our birthdays, so we didn't celebrate them. The Wilson family wanted to give me a special birthday to remember. They surprised me at the restaurant with a chocolate cake, a loud birthday song, and multiple gifts. It was cheesy, but I loved it.

Even though the Wilson family was doing everything possible to make me feel welcomed at their home, I still felt very distant. Most of the time, I went directly to my room after entering into the house. Due to my past trauma, I wanted to stay out of the way as much as possible.

I didn't want the Wilson family to become annoyed with me and kick me out of their home. I guess it was fear for me. Fear that one day this family would get sick of me being there and send me back to Pleasant Grove. I didn't want that to happen, so I tried not to be noticed. Even when they asked me about my day, I only responded with "It was good." Or "It was cool." I didn't know what to do. I just kept to myself.

I wasn't even comfortable enough to get food from the fridge while someone was in the kitchen. I would typically wait until everyone else was in their rooms for the night. When I lived in St. Louis, my aunt and other people I stayed with hid their good food in their rooms, or they would scold you for taking something from the fridge.

The Wilson family noticed these things and were upset. They weren't upset that I was taking food, but they were upset because I felt like I could only do it when they weren't around. They knew it stemmed from the past, so they sat down with me one night. Angela and Walter reassured me that this is my house too and that whatever was in the fridge was mine too.

They also told me that they asked about my day, because they genuinely cared. I told them that I still felt uncomfortable, and shared my concerns. I didn't want to become successful in life and have someone tell me that I only made it because the Wilson family came into my life and helped me. I felt that I was already on the right path in life before meeting them.

Angela responded, "I thought you didn't care what people think? You and I both know that you would have been successful without us, but we're here together and that's what matters. Not what other people think."

They assured me that they wanted that connection in my life. Angela told me that I had already been through enough hardships in my life, and they wanted to make my life less difficult than what it had been. I sensed their concern, and I sensed that they were coming from a genuine place inside of their hearts.

We didn't have a picture-perfect family in the Wilson house, but I loved it because it was real. We had fights like any other family. We cried together, we laughed together and we grew together as a family. I started seeing them as *my* family.

My mother was a bit sad at this time, because the Wilson family gave me the things that she wished she was able to but never could. She was afraid that by accepting the new family as my own, I would disown the family I already had. I made sure my mother knew that I only had one mom, and her position could not be replaced.

Angela and Walter were like a mom and dad to me, but I could never replace my mom's position or my family's position. To me, adding more people to my life didn't mean eliminating those I already had. I told her that I have a big family now, and I love all of them together. No one's getting eliminated or replaced. Everyone comes together as a family.

I didn't know it yet, but this same way of thinking would carry on to my career as a police officer. I didn't enter the police force and forget about my neighborhood or eliminate the community from my life. I simply added police to the family I already had. I have one big family in my eyes, and I care about everyone in it.

* * *

I officially made a full transfer from Townview High School to Dallas Lutheran School for the 2011-2012 school year. I was confused when I entered Dallas Lutheran on my first day of school and there were no metal detectors set up at the front entrance. I thought that I was early, because in every school I had attended, we had metal detectors and searches of our bags upon entering the school building.

I asked Principal Nitz about the metal detectors, and he seemed more confused than I was. He simply told me that they did not have metal detectors at the school. It was strange to me. It wasn't the norm in my head, but I eventually accepted it as the new norm.

My school life was everything that Principal Nitz told me it would be. It was hard. I had a loaded schedule, and I had to double down on school courses. I had nine classes, and two more online classes on top of that. Not to mention, I was the Varsity Basketball Team Captain. I would go from schoolwork, to practice, and back to schoolwork. I typically didn't go to bed each night until about 2 or 3 am. I felt exhausted, but my internal drive to be successful kept me going in life.

I was well received by everyone I encountered. I felt like I was accepted. When I played basketball in the past, no one came to my basketball games. I felt like I didn't have any support or anyone to cheer me on and that the crowd was against me. But now, it was different. My family came to my basketball games, my classmates cheered for me, and people from my past came to support me. Sgt. Padilla from JROTC at Townview, my old principal from Townview, and old friends from Townview and Franklin came to support me.

I used to feel upset in the past that my family wasn't with me, but that all changed. When I looked towards the crowd and saw my family, friends and classmates cheering for me, I no longer felt like my family wasn't there with me. My family was here! They were loud and proud.

I started seeing the bigger picture in life. The same kid who was once bullied on a daily basis now had a whole crowd cheering for him. The table had been turned for me. I had created a new life for myself in Texas. God had given me a bigger family and a large support system with people who truly cared about me. I used that energy to power me through all of the challenges I encountered that year.

I managed to power my way through the school year with my double classes, Varsity Team Captain responsibilities, and school life challenges. At the end of the school year, I won the Balanced Life Award from my church because of my ability to balance the many responsibilities I had that year with school, sports and home life. After conquering the school year, I started to prepare for my high school graduation. My graduation was a big deal because not too long ago, I thought that school had been taken away from me forever.

I took a step back and admired how God flipped my entire life and gave everything back to me in better condition. My mom, brother, grandmother and great aunt all planned to attend my high school graduation. Angela and Walter had paid for my family's travel expenses. This was a big moment for me because it was the first time that my family would meet the Wilson family in person. It was like a crossover episode on the Disney channel when the main characters from two different shows are in one show together. I was nervous and excited at the same time.

When the Wilson family and the Sims family met each other, it went better than I expected. In all honesty, I don't think I really had many expectations. I just waited to see if both sides would mix well, because I loved them both. I wanted them to like each other and come together as a family.

Justin walked into the Wilson house, and Walter immediately went up to him and said, "I want to shake your hand, because you did an amazing job raising him."

My brother responded, "Nah, he's always been a good kid. He did that. I just made sure my little bro was always safe."

Walter didn't take any credit away from Justin because, in fact, he did a great job. I speak so highly of my brother because I wouldn't be here without him. Justin protected me so much, and he ensured

I made it through every challenge in life when I was with him. Justin sacrificed a lot for me, and he always had my back no matter what problem I faced. Justin always said that if I had a problem in life, then it was his problem too. That's why so many people were anxious to meet him. They wanted to meet the man who made sure I made it to this point in my life.

I looked around the house and saw my grandmother playing with Owen, Grayson and Lucy. It was a heart-warming moment. The Wilson kids instantaneously connected to my grandmother, and she loved them back. I saw my mother speaking with Angela, sharing smiles and laughs. It was a perfect family moment.

It was the night before my high school graduation, and I decided to sleep with my family at the hotel. Once I was alone with my mom, brother, and grandmother at the hotel, they shared their thoughts about the Wilson family. My brother said that his only concern at the beginning was if the Wilson family would fully accept me in their household. Justin said that he was a little skeptical about this until he walked into the living room at the Wilson house and saw the big portrait of me with the family. Once he saw that giant portrait in the living room, he knew I was a part of the family now. I reassured him that the Wilson family was great to me and accepted me into their family with open arms. My grandmother emphasized on what a beautiful family the Wilsons were and how much she enjoyed spending time with their kids.

My mom spent the whole night sitting in the bed, writing. She looked very sad and yet focused. I saw her wipe her tears away a few times, but she told me that she would give me what she wrote at my graduation. My mom told me that she didn't have money for a graduation gift and that she wasn't a great writer, but she knew how much I valued handwritten things from people. My mother decided to make a handwritten card that I was going to open up on my graduation day.

Graduation day was a special day for me. I got to see both of my families together, and they both got to share a key moment in my life. My name was called, and I walked across the stage and received my high school diploma. I had worked so hard to get back into school, and I had reached the finish line.

Once I had my high school diploma in hand, I attempted to make my way back to my seat. My grandmother stopped me in my tracks, gave me a big hug and said, "I'm so proud of you."

Then I looked at the stands and saw Angela and my mom hugging each other and crying together. The moment couldn't have been more perfect for me. I felt proud.

After hundreds of photos and "I'll miss you" handshakes and hugs with classmates, my mother approached me and gave me the card she had written for me. My brother also had a handwritten card for me. Both of their cards meant a lot to me, because I knew neither one of them were fans of writing notes or letters. I waited to read the cards until I got back home after graduation.

I read my brother's card first. He spoke about how proud he was of me, and the difficult path we both endured together to be where we are in life. Justin told me that he hoped our journey in life together never ends. His card meant a lot to me, and it made a bigger impact on me knowing that he wrote it just for me.

I opened my mother's card next. Up to this point, my mother had never mentioned anything about her abandoning us when I was 12 years old. Every time the subject would be brought up, my mother would change the subject or pretend like it didn't exist or act like it never happened. In this card, she finally addressed it.

My mother wrote that there wasn't a day that went by when she didn't regret what she did by leaving us. When I read that line, it felt like my heart dropped. I instantaneously started crying and read the rest. It was like the young Brion inside of me was brought back to life. That same young Brion who loved his mom and was heartbroken when she left.

While reading the card, I felt like I connected with the pain that she felt. Here I was focused on my feelings and never thought to myself that maybe she wasn't ready to accept what she had done in the past. She wanted to forget the mistake of abandoning her children. Who was I to hold someone to the memory they regretted the most and repented for?

My mother addressed how she had to seek mental help after her actions and how lost she was at the time after leaving us. She didn't excuse herself from her actions. She just brought light to her feelings, and I respected that the most. I don't hold anything against her because of my faith and who I am inside. I couldn't refuse forgiveness to her for her wrongs in the past and then ask God to forgive me for the wrongs in my life. I had to forgive to receive forgiveness.

I loved her. I love her.

My mother's card finally addressed something that I wanted to hear from her, which was her acknowledgement of what happened in the past. When she left, I was seriously hurt and broken inside. God restored me. When I read the card and saw that my mother was also hurt, I trusted God would do the same restoration for her.

My mom also addressed all of the friends and family members that were there to show love to me at my graduation. My mother wrote that she remembered as a kid, I always wanted friends, and now I had so many friends in my life. My mother wrote that seeing my smile and my success in life was a true blessing to her and that it should be a reminder to me on how far I had come in life. God had given me a new way of life and a whole new team of people that cared for me.

I ran up to my mother after reading the card. We spent the whole night hugging and crying together. It was a long and emotional night for both of us.

* * *

My family returned back to their home states the next day, and it was time for me to prepare for college.

After graduating high school, I went to Oklahoma State University for a year and then transferred to the University of Texas at Arlington. I'm purposely skipping over my college life experience for now, and you'll see why at the end of this book.

During the summer breaks and after my college classes, I worked with the YMCA as a camp counselor and group leader. I loved my job, and the kids there loved me. I always wanted to make an impact on a kid's life in a positive fashion. I grew up as a kid without too many positive male role models in my life, so I decided that I would be that positive male leader that I wished I had. I didn't know at the time that working with kids would give me most of the skills I needed in the future to work with unruly adults as a police officer. Adults often times act like big kids themselves.

At the end of my first year with the YMCA, I was voted camp counselor of the year by the kids. I had an amazing three years working for the YMCA and positively impacting the lives of various kids from different backgrounds. After my time with the YMCA and finishing my college degree, it was time for me to move on to my career. The kids and the staff members were sad to see me leave, but they were happy that I was finally going to follow my dreams. They knew that I aspired to be something else in life. I wanted to be a police officer.

I always get the question of what inspired me to be a police officer since I had a few bad run-ins with officers in my past. Simply put, I wanted to make a difference.

I used the memories of Officer Burt, the cop in Davis's neighborhood, and the officer who bad-mouthed my aunt as examples of the type of cop I *didn't* want to be. I used the memories of my teachers at Townview, who were former police officers and domestic violence counselors, as examples to show me the impact on a kid's life that I wanted to make. I also used the memories of the police officers who ran the Dallas Explorers program as examples to show me the positive impact I wanted to make in the world as an officer.

I felt that we needed more good police officers in the world like those officers from the explorers program. I basically wanted to be the change that I had wanted to see. So often in my past, the only time I encountered police officers was when they took a family member to jail. I wanted to show my face for more than just the times I had to make an arrest or take enforcement action. I wanted to be an officer that did his job, but also reached out to the community. My friends and family called me crazy when I told them that my dream was to bring together the community and police officers. I felt that both should be together instead of separate. I believed that we both needed each other to exist.

That was my goal and it felt right. I always felt like I didn't choose law enforcement. God led me to this career. After many years, my time came to join the police force and step up to the plate.

Mentors in my life had advised me that the job of a police officer would not be an easy task and that I may not get a warm welcome when I put that badge on. They told me that my badge would be "heavy." I assured them that it wouldn't be the first time in my life enduring hardships and that my dream was worth more than the struggles I'd encounter. God's plan for me was worth more. I was ready. After all, someone has to step up to the plate. My time had come to step up and make an impact.

The day I called the recruiting office of the Dallas Police Department, I was scared out of my mind. I was nervous and had no idea what I was signing up for. I was sitting in a parking garage, just staring at my phone until I finally got up the courage to dial the number.

The recruiter gave me a date to come down for the initial testing. I made it to the testing center, and the place was packed with cadet hopefuls. Everyone at the testing center had aspirations to be a police officer but not everyone could make it. I approached the front table of the testing center, and one of the recruiting officers reviewing the entrance exams started looking through my fifty-page application packet.

The packet included everything the government wanted to know about you and your background. They wanted to know about the information you were willing to share and the information that you may be hiding from them. The questions in the packet referenced basic information, financial history, relationships, criminal history and just about everything else you could think to ask. The application in itself was a bit exhausting, but I completed it.

The officer reviewing my application stopped at one of the pages and said, "You don't have your father's info here."

I told him that I never knew my father and had no information about him. The officer told me to go figure out the information and return back next time with the information completed. He told me that there'd be another testing in a few months.

I was waiting for him to say he was joking, but he handed me back my packet and said, "Next!"

I could've quit right there. I could've walked away due to his rude comment and said, "If this is who is representing this department, I don't want to work here." Instead, his comment fueled something else inside of me. I thought to myself, "I have journeyed too far in my life to let someone block me from my goals now."

I turned back towards the officer and told him, "My father has never been in my life and never will be. That's who he is. You're really going to allow a man who has never been in my life make an impact on it today?"

I was stern and just stared at him. The officer stared back for what felt like an eternity.

He then slowly nodded his head and said, "Okay, fine."

The officer took the application packet and said everything else looked good. Maybe he admired that I didn't back down or maybe he was just tired of me holding up his line causing a scene, but either way, he took the packet.

The entire process, before I was actually accepted in the police academy, took about three months. It involved physical fitness tests, lie detector tests, psychological examinations, medical examinations, academic tests, and deep background checks. After three long months, I was still waiting on a phone call from Dallas PD.

I lived by myself at this time in a small one-bedroom apartment. I was still taking classes at Brookhaven College and finishing up my Associate's Degree in Criminal Justice.

I was on my way home from class one day when I received the phone call. I didn't recognize the number, so I answered with caution.

The voice on the phone said, "This is Detective Pierce with Dallas Police. Are you still interested in becoming a police officer?"

I responded, "Yes sir, I am."

He told me, "Congratulations, you've been accepted into the Police Academy Class #349."

I was lost for words. I just remember saying thank you and sitting in the parking lot for about thirty minutes just thinking about my life journey up to this point.

I didn't have much time to prepare, since I was the last recruit to be accepted in Class #349. I only had about a week to mentally and physically prepare before the official police academy started. The Dallas Police Academy is about nine and a half months long, which is the longest police academy in the nation, but it gives some of the best training a recruit can receive. I knew that the police academy wouldn't be easy, and I knew that it would take everything inside of me to make it through. Even though I knew it would be difficult, I was ready to start the next chapter of my life.

I kept thinking about how I was one step closer to my dream of being a police officer. It felt so surreal. I eventually received my congratulations letter from Dallas PD, and it was one of the proudest moments I ever had. I sat on the floor of my apartment and stared at the letter for about an hour straight. I couldn't get a grasp on the moment. I was in shock. Everything was starting to become real for me. I had just been accepted to the police academy, and now my dream was becoming a reality.

CHAPTER 10:

CODE OF HONOR

I officially started the Dallas Police Academy on Dec 2, 2015 with no knowledge of what was going to happen. On the first day, I arrived at the police academy wearing a suit, as the acceptance letter had instructed us to do. I was scared out of my mind. The worst type of fear is the unknown, because your head starts to create one million scenarios of possible outcomes.

The first day consisted of multiple speeches from various police officers. A police instructor came into the room and told us that no one in the room (referring to the cadets) was his brother or sister. He stated that we were all "hopefuls" who were granted the opportunity to earn a badge with meaning to it. The instructor said this academy class would be our attempt to one day be called a police officer.

He gave a very "heartwarming" speech, telling us that most of us weren't going to make it through the police academy. He said the ones that quit would be the ones we didn't need in the first place. The instructor assured us that he would mentally and physically break us. It felt like I was back at JCLC military camp all over again, with all the yelling, workouts, drills and high levels of discipline.

The academy instructors tried to be as harsh and difficult as possible, but this was nothing new to me. Everything they threw at me, I had already seen it twice before in my life. I was ready for it. It wasn't my first time being yelled at, wasn't my first time being called names, wasn't my first time having to prove something to others, and it wasn't my first time digging deep inside of myself to overcome challenges. The way I saw it, God brought me here for a reason, and I refused to stop until that mission was completed. I felt like everything I had been through in my life prepared me for the police academy.

Word got around the academy that I went to a private school my senior year of high school, so I earned the nickname, "Private School." I wasn't too fond of the nickname since it kind of pinned me to all of the private school stereotypes and predisposed narratives that weren't true. But that's the police academy! Everyone in the academy had a nickname that they didn't like. The goal of the undesired nickname was to hit the triggers inside of you and see if you were mentally strong enough to endure what was thrown at you without breaking apart or losing your cool.

Throughout the academy, we endured a lot of hardships. Besides the normal assortment of physical exercises, fighting drills, and weapons training, there was mental training as well. We went through a lot of mental-health training, de-escalation training, and academic tests every other week. You had to be physically strong and mentally capable to do the job. They put us through a lot of real-life scenarios and graded us on every move we made.

Our class consisted of twenty-nine cadets, and I respected each one of them because they were pushing through just like me. Our recruit class was made up of different races, genders and cultural backgrounds. Despite our differences, our class clicked. I even met my best friends, Shepard and Ramirez, whom I connected with the most. My best friends in the police academy constantly motivated me to power through when I was mentally and physically drained, and I did the same for them during their moments of weakness. We were a team.

Shepard was a big country boy from the great state of Mississippi. He stood tall at 6 foot 4 inches and weighed about 265 pounds. Before entering the police academy, Shepard played college football at Mississippi State. He joined the police force to make a difference.

We sat next to each other in the academy classroom and quickly became friends. Shepard and I built our friendship through the many challenges of the academy. We relied on each and pushed each other to the next level when times got tough.

Ramirez came from the state of Alabama and proudly represented his Mexican roots. Ramirez joined the academy to make a change in the community. He had a natural desire to protect people.

We were friends inside and outside of the academy. The demanding nature of the academy caused us to rely on each other more. The academy made our friendship stronger. I am proud to say that we are all still friends to this day.

On the first day of the police academy, the instructor sat us all down in a classroom and told us that there would be a day during the Police Academy that we would need to answer two simple questions in our head: "Why am I here?" and "Do I really want to be a police officer?"

These questions seemed easy enough, but they held more weight than we thought. These two questions had the power to break you in the police academy, especially at moments of mental exhaustion and weakness. The instructor stated that if you could not answer these questions on the day your mind was challenged and wanted to break and quit, then you would not make it.

My day for these questions came midway through the police academy when we were doing weapon training outside. I can't emphasize this enough, but the weather was horrible, a freezing temperature with high winds and pouring rain. It was a perfect weather recipe to break a recruit. I was soaking wet, and my hands were frozen solid.

Even with these factors, the instructors were not letting up on the military-style training. They continued pushing us and going back-to-back-to-back with drills. I couldn't feel my hands, face, or legs due to the freezing weather. Then one of the recruits became bold enough to ask the instructor if we could go inside and warm up a bit since we were all frozen solid.

The instructor sarcastically responded with, "I'm sorry if it's too cold for you. Sure you can go inside. You want me to bring you some hot chocolate too while you're in there warming up?"

His face then quickly turned serious again and yelled, "Get back in line! You don't get to control the weather in this job! We train in everything! Now, Mr. 'Let's Go inside for a bit' just earned y'all another set of drills!"

The instructor meant every word of it.

We went back-to-back with more drills, and my numb hands ended up dropping the magazine to my gun during reload drills. It felt like the world stopped. I was already physically hurting from the climate and the drills, and then the instructor made his way over to me.

He asked me, "Did you just drop your magazine with your ammo in it? Congratulations, you're dead now because you failed to successfully reload. If this training is a little too tough for you, you know the road home."

His words got inside of my head that day. I don't exactly know why but they did. Maybe it was due to mental or physical exhaustion, but I thought about quitting that day. The weather was horrendous and the constant drills started mentally draining me.

When you're mentally and physically exhausted, you're at your most vulnerable state to be broken.

I said to myself, "Maybe it would be easier to quit and go home right now. I can return home, be comfortable in my own home and find another career. Why am I here? Do I really want to be here? Do I really want to be a cop?"

The instructor then dismissed us for lunch. He told us that some of us needed to rethink our careers.

I slowly walked to my car in the parking lot with the little feeling I still had left in my body. I sat in my car and just stared aimlessly at the dashboard.

I thought to myself, "I could drive home right now. I could forget this police academy ever happened and leave right now."

These thoughts circled through my head until another side of me started to speak up. My journey in life started to flash before my eyes. Everything I had endured and been through started to come to me. It was like God brought these memories to my head to motivate me and to keep me strong during my moment of doubt. This was a moment where I struggled to see the light, but God brought me light.

I started thinking to myself, "Don't forget how far you've come, what you've had to endure and overcome in your life, what you strive to be, and the people who stand with you. How would I look going to schools and speaking to kids, trying to motivate them to be strong and overcome challenges if I quit right now?"

I felt like I had a whole community on my back. I felt like I was representing something stronger and greater than myself. I had to take a stand for reasons beyond myself and serve a greater purpose in this world. I had to make it and inspire people to do the same.

I wanted people to say, "He made it, so I need to do the same," and not "He failed, so I guess I can too."

I stared at my reflection in my rearview mirror, and I answered those two questions the instructor had given us at the beginning of the police academy: Why are you here? Do you really want to be a police officer?

I said to myself, "I'm here because I'm supposed to be here. I'm doing this for more than just myself. I have people looking up to me. I'm not a quitter. I'm a survivor and I'm a fighter. My past highlights that, and now my present will highlight that again. The fight is never over, and I'm here. I want to be a police officer."

I knew that if I quit and went home, I would be in a lot more pain than what I felt at the moment. So instead, I sat in my car, ate my lunch, and went right back to it. The instructor even gave a slight smile when I came back from lunch and stepped on the drill line.

He said, "That's what I like to see. Determination. Let's get back to it!"

When my mindset was on the right track, everything felt easy to me after that. I knew that no matter what the police academy threw at me, I was ready for it.

* * *

One day at the police academy, we were mentally preparing for taser training. At the end of the classroom training, everyone had to get zapped by the taser for a five-second duration. Let's just say that I wasn't looking forward to that part. I patiently waited in the classroom for the instructors to prepare everything for the practical portion of the taser class.

A group of high-school students were taking a tour of the police academy. I looked out in the hallway and saw Townview High School t-shirts and sweaters—my old high school. At the front of the group, I saw my former Criminal Justice teacher, Mr. Perez. He locked eyes with me and quickly made his way over. We were both surprised to see each other, and I was excited to see one of my favorite teachers from Townview.

Mr. Perez asked me about my academy experience and then asked me to speak to his students. He told me that the students were Freshmen at Townview Law Magnet. The police instructors agreed that it was okay for me to speak to the students, and the instructors set up a room for us. I walked to the front of the classroom and saw all those Freshmen faces looking at me.

I introduced myself to the class, and the kids were shocked that I had attended Townview Law Magnet. The students couldn't believe that I had attended their school and was now in the police academy. Other students were shocked that I had lived in their same neighborhood. While speaking to the students, I saw the younger version of me in their faces. I remembered when I had visited the Dallas Police Academy while at Townview, and now here I was, an official recruit.

At the time, I was still chasing my dreams, so I couldn't say too much to them for inspiration. I spoke to them about the importance of school and the work ethic needed in life to make things happen. I then answered one million questions that the students had after my speech.

"What made you want to be a cop? Did you have Mr. Washington as your History teacher? Where did you stay at in Pleasant Grove? Are you scared to be a cop? Do y'all really like coffee and donuts?"

I think the "question-asking" part was their favorite. I can honestly say that it was my favorite part too. I had their curiosity, and I felt more relaxed. I wasn't even a cop yet, but I could already feel myself making a difference in kids' lives.

After speaking with the students, Mr. Perez pulled me to the side of the room and gave me a speech that motivated me even more.

He said, "You gotta make it. All of these kids are looking up to you. You come from the same neighborhood as they do. They need someone like you out there protecting them. You're cut from the same cloth. Don't quit."

I felt every word he said to me. Those words struck me and reminded me that I had kids looking up to me as their role model. They needed me out there in the world. I had to finish! I then nodded my head in agreement with Mr. Perez and gave him one last goodbye.

A police instructor then came in the room and told me, "Private School, it's time to get tazed. Let's go!"

I walked back to the classroom with my fellow academy recruits, and the instructor called me into the training room to be exposed to the taser. I was then hit with Zeus's lightning bolt. Once feeling came back to my body, I reentered the classroom and the other recruits started cheering.

We had a strong support system in our class. We always had each other's back, and we weren't going to let anyone quit. With every hardship we endured in the police academy together, it made our bond even stronger.

With our strong bond growing each day, I got to learn more and more about each person in my academy class. I felt blessed to have the opportunity to meet so many amazing people before they put on their badges. I learned their backstories in life, in the same way that you are reading this book and learning about me beyond my badge. You're learning who I am and where I come from, and that's the same thing I got to do in the police academy with the other recruits. I met a lot of the police officers before they were even able to call themselves police officers.

We were all different shapes, sizes, colors and cultural backgrounds, but we all clicked. My academy classmates were from all over the United States. We had recruits from Mississippi, Louisiana, New York, Alabama, Minnesota and California. We had recruits who were former teachers, college students, NFL hopefuls, correctional officers, military, and even an ice-cream delivery driver. We came from so many unique backgrounds, but our willingness to protect and serve the community brought us all together.

After taser day, everything else felt like a flash to me. The remaining months of the academy flew by with more challenges and hardships of their own, but I made it. We made it. We unfortunately lost about three cadets during the process, but most of us made it to the end. The academy was exhausting, but there was no better feeling than running through the finish line.

We officially made it to our badge pinning ceremony after nine and a half months of training in the police academy. Earning the right to wear a badge put a sense of honor inside of me. All of the work I put into the training was about to pay off.

In the police academy, there are two different ceremonies at the end of the year. There's the badge-pinning ceremony and then there's an actual graduation. Once again, I was going to have another proud day to look forward to in life. I had accomplished what many aren't able to do.

News quickly spread to my family back home that I had completed the police academy, and my family started preparing for another road trip to the great state of Texas. Unfortunately, everyone couldn't make it to my graduation ceremony from St. Louis, but my mom, brother, and great aunt came.

I was hurting because my grandmother promised me that she would come to my graduation, but she passed away while I was in the academy. Before I started the academy, she told me that she was proud of me, but she was scared for my safety as there were police officers being killed in the news and she didn't want me to be one of them.

I told my grandmother that I would do my job so that she could safely walk to the store and not have to worry about some knucklehead trying to rob her.

My grandmother laughed, and said, "I ain't mad at that." She told me, "I'll be there when you graduate. I promise."

It was a bittersweet moment when my family showed up for my badge-pinning ceremony, but my grandmother wasn't physically present. In a strange way, I felt like she was spiritually present with all of us. When she promised me she'd be there, I knew she meant it.

My mother, my little brother Kwame (a late addition my mom made to the family), and the Wilson family attended the first event, my badge-pinning ceremony. During the ceremony, a special person is required to pin your badge to your chest. When it was my turn, my mother stepped up, but then she stopped and turned around towards Angela and Walter. She told them that they are my family too, and she wanted them to be a part of this moment. When the badge was pinned on my chest, we all turned towards the camera and took a photo together as one big family. It was a special moment to me.

I drove home that night and called my mentor Blair, who mentored me through a program called International Student Foundation (ISF). The program gives scholarships to children who undergo the foster-care system and places mentors in their lives to help them succeed. I was never in foster-care, but they made an exception for me. I had a deep discussion with Blair that night, which he loves to repeat at different speaking events now.

I told him about the power of the badge. I told him that before I received the police badge, I thought it would make me feel powerful and provide me with great character traits. I basically thought it would give me superpowers and everything I needed to be a cop, but I didn't feel like that when I first put it on.

When I first put on the badge, I just felt the same. I just felt like me. I didn't feel like a cop or how I thought a cop would feel putting on the badge. I felt very proud to have my badge, but I didn't get any superpowers.

Then I realized that it was a very good thing that I didn't feel any different putting on the badge, because I understood that it wasn't the badge that made the man. I defined who I was inside and not the badge I put on. The police badge showed my accomplishment of making it through the police academy and what I'm supposed to represent, but it didn't define me. I define the person I want to be in life, and it's reflected on the badge I carry. Not the other way around.

I saw the badge as a mirror. Who you are will be reflected on the badge. I told him that if you were a bad person before you put on the badge, then putting on a shiny metal plate won't change that. You will be that same person but with a badge on. If you were strong and possessed good character traits before the badge, then that's who you will be after you put it on. I told him that I'm just me with a badge, and that's the positive energy I will reflect in the world.

Blair agreed with me, and he said that he was proud of me for my mental understanding of the badge. Blair said I should keep reflecting the positive traits I possessed before I even started the police academy. I mentally locked in everything I felt that night.

The next day was our actual graduation ceremony. The Wilson family, the Sims family and the Vanderlin family all came together for this special moment. It felt like another clash of the episodes in my life with everyone together in one place. I also had my mentor Blair and his wife Helen present, who were both strong supporters of me. Everyone took photos together, and it created a lasting memory in my head of a great accomplishment.

Every goal I accomplished in life always caused me to reflect on the road I had traveled to get to that point. I thought to myself that I'm the same kid who thought hope was gone in my life when my mom left. I'm the same kid who was sitting on the street curb without a place to go, without food to eat, without anyone to call on—and now I had accomplished so much in life. Life had turned around for me.

My heart was content. I felt so blessed that God had led me to this point, and I could start making a difference. I could start living my dream, and now I felt like I had something to pass on to others and inspire them to do the same.

* * *

After graduating the police academy, I was sent to work at the Southeast substation of the Dallas Police Department. Southeast included neighborhoods like Pleasant Grove, "Deep Grove," and parts of south Dallas. The southeast subdivision had a reputation of being the toughest sector in Dallas. Southeast led the city in highest crime rate, and it had the highest drop out rate for new recruits. They told us that the new officers stationed at Southeast would be pushed the hardest, and they meant every word of it. The training at Southeast felt harder than the police academy at times, but I loved every minute of it.

Southeast was the same police station where I was a Dallas Police Explorer, so I already had a connection with the area. I was back in my old neighborhood of Pleasant Grove, but this time I was a cop. Southeast taught me so much in a short amount of time. I had three great trainers who taught me what I needed to know to survive on the streets and how to become a better officer. The combination of these trainers alongside my background experience, allowed me to grow into the cop I wanted to be in life.

My first trainer had five years of experience and taught me how to properly build a connection with the community. We visited recreational centers, neighborhood parks and talked to random people in the street. He emphasized the importance of a good community relationship.

My second trainer had twenty-seven years of experience and taught me how to keep my job as an officer. He emphasized the importance of getting all of my paperwork done on time and making the right decision on a police call.

My third trainer had about seventeen years of experience and was by far the toughest. He taught me patience, resilience and how to be a one-man team. He was the type of trainer who you couldn't please. Everything I did was wrong. If I chose the left door, he'd say that I should've chosen the right door. If I wrote in black ink, he'd say you should've written in blue. You get the point. He was that type of trainer.

At the end of my training, I used each lesson I learned to make myself into the best officer I could be. I never received a complaint from my supervisor about incomplete reports, because I handled my business like my second phase trainer taught me. I also took care of the entire call when cover officers weren't available to assist me, like my third trainer taught me. And I received praises from the community for interacting with them and making time to check on people and local businesses, like my first phase trainer taught me.

Southeast Dallas was a tough area to work, but you'd be surprised at the high number of people who were actually happy to see us patrolling the neighborhood. Citizens always told me that they were happy to see police officers keeping the area safe. This came from every racial, religious, and cultural background.

My partner and I made time during the shift to go to different rec centers to hang out with the kids in the neighborhood. I even visited my old schools on my off days to speak to the students. I wanted interactions beyond what my duties were as an officer. I knew in order to bring community and police together, I would need to go into the community to make the difference. I always said that if I can at least change one person's life, I was content with that, but the goal is to impact everyone.

I had officially embraced my new life as a police officer and maintained the vision I had for the community. I visited Franklin Middle School and Townview High School to speak to kids about the road to success. I spoke to them about making good decisions in life and fighting through adversity to make it in life. I also spoke at multiple events with ISF (International Student Foundation) since I was an alumni member. In ISF, I spoke with college students who had been in the foster-care system. I shared my life's journey with them and spoke about the tools that helped me reach this point in life. I also journeyed with Orphan Outreach to participate in a mission trip to Guatemala where we visited multiple orphanages in the country and gave them a Christmas celebration.

I constantly tried to make an impact when I could. I wanted to live beyond my basic role as an officer. I am the same homeless kid who sat on the curb and had nothing. The same kid who was told by his uncle that he'd be nothing. Now I was an officer making a difference, defying the odds, and travelling around the world to make a true impact.

* * *

After almost four years with Dallas Police Department, I transferred to another one. I enjoyed my time with Dallas PD, but it was time to move on to the next stage in my life. In August of 2018, I transferred to the Frisco Police Department, which was a complete change in scenery and culture.

Frisco and Dallas are total opposites of each other, like day and night. Dallas was an established metropolitan area that constantly had high activity for police responses. Frisco was a rural city that aspired to be a big city. When I initially joined, Frisco had a lot of farmland, cows getting loose and roaming the streets, and not too many police calls. Frisco also had a lot of construction sites spread throughout the city. Frisco quickly became one of the fastest-growing cities, and I wanted to be a part of that growth.

When I changed to Frisco PD, I considered whether or not it was the right decision. I started thinking that it was probably a bad idea, because the culture of the community and the department was so different from what I was accustomed. Frisco Police Department did their best to welcome me into my new role, but I still had difficulty blending in.

I thought to myself, "They don't have anyone like me here, so maybe I should go back to Dallas." That same reasoning for wanting to leave was the reason I stayed in Frisco: "They don't have anyone like me here."

I felt like the city needed someone with a mindset and background like mine. If I didn't stay, then who would be there to make that representation? It's easy to complain about a problem, but it's harder to be the change you want to see and truly make a difference. I became the officer I wanted to see. I made the decision to stay, and the job started to change for me in a positive way.

Frisco, the community, the citizens, the police department and the officers I worked with were very welcoming. Most of the officers in Frisco were from other agencies, so they were able to understand the initial feelings I had with being a transfer officer. I interacted with citizens in the community, who would always show how thankful they were for our presence.

On random traffic stops in the city, some of the citizens would just stare at me.

They would look at me, smile and say, "I'm glad you're here. Frisco is definitely growing for the better."

To some, I was the first black officer they had seen in the city, but I wasn't only defined by being a black officer. I was an officer who reflected a positive example of the badge that I carried. That is what they respected the most. I represented my job, culture and background in a positive light.

When I made the decision to stay in Frisco, everything seemed to flow a lot smoother in the city. I've been here for three years now and don't have any plans of leaving anytime soon. I can wholeheartedly say that the thing I love the most about working in Frisco is the opportunity to make a great impact with a developing city. I have the chance to be a part of history here.

I always lived with the principle of life that there is a code of honor that I needed to uphold. I've been blessed enough to have worked with amazing officers who I consider to be my brothers and sisters. I have love for the community and the police force. Just like when my two families merged in the past, I didn't eliminate one group to be with another group. I simply added to the family. I love both the officers I serve with and the communities I serve.

Is it tough to endure at times? Yes. Did I give up hope on my dream? No. Adversity is not new to me. Proving myself isn't new to me. Fighting each day for my dream isn't new to me. I have travelled a long road to make it to this point in life.

My job as a police officer isn't an easy one. I take heat every day. I constantly deal with things like hurtful comments, name-calling, physical pain, exhaustion, stress, and everything else you can imagine, but I don't let that change who I am. I remain strong despite the hate I sometimes receive in my job.

During a police shift, I was called the N-word by a white man and an Uncle Tom by a black woman all in the same day before I was in the room for more than five seconds. My presence alone caused them to say those words. I was judged before I even said anything.

I took the time to address the predisposed judgment that both sides had of me. I challenged them to connect with who I am. Whether they were initially judging me based on my skin tone or simply the uniform I wore, I wanted them to see more than what their eyes or what their prejudgments told them to feel about me. In the end, they respected me more.

Their judgments of me gave more emphasis to my dream of "bridging the gap." I made it a practice to speak with people when there was down time in my job. I would stop by parks, storefronts, schools, and just random places to have conversations with people in the community. This allowed them to see me in a different scope other than the moments when I had to make an arrest. They were able to meet the man that my badge reflected.

Hopefully when you see me, hear my story, and feel the words I say, you can also see the badge that reflects that image as well. I didn't let my past hold me back from being the best me that I could be. I took my past and let it build myself to who I am today. I chose the path of a police officer for my life in order to make the biggest impact I felt that I could. In my head, this was always God's plan for my life.

I use everything from my past to effectively do my job now. I smile when I put on my uniform, because I made it. I made to where I was destined to be. If a homeless 12-year-old kid from St. Louis can do it, you definitely can! Use everything to make it and to make a positive impact in your life. Never let your past hold you back from the future. You have to go for it. That's all the motivation you really need!

CHAPTER 11:
REASONS BEYOND MYSELF

I continue to work for the Frisco Police Department. I continue to wake up and put on my uniform with pride. My job brings satisfaction to me, because I am in a position to impact the lives of many people in our city. My vision for the future is to impact many cities across the nation.

While chasing my goals in life, my family continues to support me along the way. My mother has reentered my life with more love than ever before, and Justin continues to protect me as always. I continue to spend time with the new friends and family that have entered my life. They are proud of who I have become, because they know where I come from. I have journeyed a long way to this position.

I started off as a kid that was raised in an environment that was meant for me to fail. Now life is different for me.

The neighborhood I live in is the total opposite of where I was raised. Some days I return home, look around and start to live inside of my head. I start thinking about where I came from and where I am now.

I have the basic essentials in life, and I no longer have to worry about where my next meal will come from. My life completely flipped around from living on the streets to being in a uniform with a badge. It still shocks me that I came from living a "survival life," and now I'm in a better position where I don't have to worry anymore. I worked hard for this. I fought hard for the success I wanted in this world.

Now I have one giant family, a large group of friends, a stable home and a stable job. I'm also impacting the lives of others as well. It may seem like an abrupt ending, but the ending isn't here yet. I'm still here and I'm still accomplishing my goals in this world.

That's where I am right now in life. It may not seem like much to some, but it has been a long journey for me. This book wasn't originally supposed to be a "book." Writing this book started about seven years ago as a mental-health exercise. Throughout my years, I've struggled with depression, anxiety and PTSD from everything that had occurred in my past.

Writing is an outlet for me. Writing is freedom to me. I've always enjoyed it. It is a way for me to liberate all of the thoughts in my head from the past and put them onto paper. I had decided to confront my fears by going face to face with my past so that I could move forward with my life.

I was supposed to delete everything after I was done writing it, but for some reason I didn't do it. Something inside of me held onto the writings I had started seven years ago. Now I use my writings as a way to connect with others.

I was also influenced to write this book from my involvement with students and other peers. The more I worked with the youth and spoke at events with students and adults about my past, it was astonishing to me how many kids and adults related to the same background and struggles that I went through in life. In my head, this book had to be written so that a connection could be made to everyone with similar struggles in life.

If I had to give a piece of advice to someone who has experienced or is experiencing a similar background to mine, my advice would be to use your struggles to empower you and not to overpower you. I used the struggles of my past to build me into a stronger person. My past tried to destroy who I was, but instead, I let it build on who I already was. If I allowed the past to overpower me, I definitely wouldn't be here right now to share my past with you.

I will list a few things that helped me through the difficult times I had with the past. As I told you before, I dealt with many mental battles from everything that happened. Those past experiences created hardships in my head with lasting effects. These tips are what helped me get a handle/grip on my life.

(1) Find Your Muse to Life. Use positive forms of expressions to channel your struggles. Writing was mine. I was able to find a

quiet space and channel depression and challenges into words. For you it may be music, art, exercise, etc.

(2) Find Time to Focus on Your Mental Health. We live in a very fast-paced world now. Sometimes we move so quickly and address so many tasks in life at once that we forget to make time for ourselves. I do this myself from time to time. Whether we want to accept it or not, the brain, the mind and the body needs a break. Take time to address areas in your life, outside of the fast-paced world, that may need improvements.

(3) One Step at a Time. You can't solve all your problems in one day. As much as I would personally like to do this, it was a long road for me. It took a lot of self-reflection and acknowledgment of past struggles to understand I needed to confront my past issues. So, I wrote out the problems I was dealing with, and I addressed them one by one. Slowly but surely, changes were being made to my life and people could see that, but more importantly, I personally felt better myself. Progress feels good.

(4) Find a Community Base. Find people that you can confide in who can help you through the struggles you may feel. Whether it be friends, family, the church, community groups, or even therapy, find what best works for you.

(5) Know That You Are Worth More In Life. As a kid who experienced a lot of bullying and mental abuse from peers and family, know that you are more than the negative words of others. You are

not defined by the outlooks of people that find joy in bullying or mentally/verbally abusing another. God sees you as so much more in life.

(6) Fight through the Negativity. I learned a long time ago that people will talk about you no matter what. Once you make your rise to the top, "haters" will naturally follow behind your success. You will hear a bunch of these haters/negative people saying whatever they can to break you and to bring you back down to their positions in life. Block out the hate. Block out the negativity and continue to fight through it. Don't let a hater or a spiteful person stop you from being great and achieving true success.

(7) Find What Makes You Happy. Finding inner peace and enjoying the little things in life makes a big difference in the way you feel. Find activities to be involved in whether it be sports, music, nature, etc.

(8) Live Beyond the "Impossible." I've heard "impossible" my entire life. I was told that there was no way a kid like me could make it out of St. Louis alive. There was no way I could make a new life in Texas. There was no way a kid like me could be a cop. There was no way I would be successful. There was no way anyone would read my book or come to listen to me speak. If I listened to these people or tried to reason with them, I would still be in the same position I was in the past. You wouldn't even be reading this book

now. I had to dream beyond these notions. I encourage you to do the same.

* * *

There are those in the world who are hurt inside so they hurt others, and then there are those who are hurt inside and never want anyone else to experience that pain. I'm the second one. I've never been the type of person who has wanted to hurt anyone. I take my past experiences as they are—a past that I had to endure. Even though my past was difficult, I don't try to transfer that pain onto another person. Instead, I use my pain to inspire others who may have had the same or similar difficulties in their lives.

I want to show people that, yes, I had a difficult past and I'm still encountering challenges every day, but I don't let it hold me down. Instead, I use it as motivation to do better in life and to be a better person. My faith plays a major role with everything in my life and the way that I think. It also has to do with the mental strength I gained by experiencing so many different challenges in my life. I had to be strong to make it to where I am now.

I use that acquired strength to impact as many as I can now with my past. When I first reached out and spoke with students, I did it to inspire them to be different than who the neighborhood may be luring them to be. I wanted them to have the mental strength that I had to learn the "hard way" to obtain. I wanted their paths to be easier than mine.

I grew up in St. Louis, and a majority of the paths the neighborhood created for us were through drugs, gangs, rappers and sports. When sports didn't work out then it was back to drugs and gangs. I want to break this cycle in the hearts and minds of kids growing up in these types of neighborhoods. I've seen it play out too often. I tell kids to live above that. I target the lives of children, because they will be the future of this world, and I'm a strong believer that impacting a child's life means so much more.

I don't even tell the students I'm a police officer until the end, because I want them to connect to who I am inside and what I've experienced first. People respect that more. I'd rather they know the man behind the job before they look at my badge. I tell them that the police path was my route in life, because I wanted to make a difference. I wanted to be the change I wanted to see in the world. I wanted to be different than the bad examples I had seen in my life. I wanted to live beyond what the streets tried to give to me.

Being out on the streets helped me realize one thing—I really didn't want to be out there. I had been stripped of clothes, money, friends, family, education, and thrown out onto the streets and told to survive. Somehow...some way...I made it through everything. That is the greatest victory you can have. When you can flip the script on life.

I went from living on the streets and having no hope to living in a good city with a job that allows me to protect others. I started off my journey undergoing bullying and not having any friends, and now I have more than I can count. Every friend or mentor I encountered in this story is still in my life and just a phone call away. I thought the concept of "family" was lost to me forever, but now I have a huge family that includes the new additions of Omari's family, Davis's family, the Wilson family, my police family, the ISF family, and so many friends that turned into my brothers and sisters.

I don't have the most fancy life, but I gained so much more when I fought against what my past was driving me to be. I put in the work and made my dreams come true. I may not be a millionaire, but I feel like one. I made it out of a system that was designed to break me, and now I'm living out my dream every day. I've accomplished many goals in life, but I still feel that God has a bigger plan for my life.

If you remember at beginning of this book, I said that I used to pray for wisdom as a kid. I wanted to be a very wise man, and now I understand when they tell you to be careful for what you pray for, because I believe that God made me just that—a wise man. He gave me the journey I took in life so that I could see different aspects of situations, different cultures of life, and different perspectives to an ongoing issue. I was shown firsthand what it was like to have nothing and what it was like to have everything.

Who knew the journey towards wisdom would be of this nature? By no means am I perfect nor have I learned everything the world has to show me, but I've learned enough to this point to pass it on to others. That's true wisdom.

My journey seemed endless at times and I had no idea where God was taking my life, but he led me to a better place. He broke my old life and made it anew. I turned my past trauma into strength. I used it as fuel to make it in life. I transformed my pain and made it into power that positively fuels me every day.

Kids from the neighborhood need positive role models in every profession possible. The more we share our success stories with the world, the more we can inspire the next generation to make it and do the same with their lives. They can see that they can be whatever they want in life, and the doors are open across the board for them to explore. I want kids to know that true success stems from you and is rooted in God.

There are millions of kids with a story just like mine, and I'm blessed to be able to share one of these stories with you. To have lived a life that I have and to be where I'm currently at in life...I'm blessed. Not everyone has made it out, but this is motivation for the youth to strive for what they want in life, by showing them someone who has made it out and lived to tell about it. This is to show those who may not know the man behind the uniform, a little bit of who I am, where I've been, and what I hope to accomplish one day with my message. I pray this story continues to spread and makes a real impact on society.

Every day it feels like I'm living in a dream world. To some, my life may just sound like a simple life. To someone like me, it's much more than that. Life was set up for me in a difficult way, and I was in a situation that was designed for me to lose. I was dealt a hand that wasn't intended for success. Success was not supposed to be in my life, but it's here.

The game changed for me. As I stated at the beginning, I'm one of those people who weren't dealt the best cards to start the game in life, but sometimes the game is played like that. The "struggle cards" I was dealt in my life actually became one of the best hands to have in the game. We can't accept our beginnings as the ending to the game.

I have a whole community on my back, and they continuously root for me in my corner. My support system is strong like that. I have to make it in life. I don't have any other choice. If I quit, I show others how to do the same. I want to inspire the youth to win in life, not quit. I want people to live beyond the challenges in life and truly live beyond themselves. I live beyond many things every day, because I choose to live that way.

I'm a man beyond my past, beyond my uniform/badge, and beyond my youth. I am beyond this because I live for reasons beyond myself. I lived past where life wanted me to be, and I ended up in a better place that God intended for me to be. That's true success in my eyes.

This book highlights a large part of my journey through life. Hopefully this book motivates you to continue the fight even if the odds seemed stacked against you. I know there are many more people like me in the world, and I hope this book will find and connect with them. My journey was a struggle that eventually led me to a better place in life. I pray the journey you are traveling does the same for you. God's work never ends.

Thank you for taking the time to learn more about me and my journey to this point in life. This book has been a blessing in itself. Hopefully I get to meet you at one of my events in the future. I'm truly thankful for all of the support!

AUTHOR'S NOTE

I pressed pause in my life to share my past, because I didn't want to be too old and forget the details of the road I've traveled. I felt this was a journey that needed to be shared.

My grandfather told me that when you refuse to tell your story, write your book, or create your song, you are cheating many people in life who may need to hear or see the very thing you're refusing to do. When you're in a position to create something special, you should do it! You have the power to influence the world in a positive way.

I used my position in life to reach out to the world. I made myself vulnerable in this book, so that I can connect to many others that can relate to my journey. This book is for them. I didn't want to cheat anyone. I could've kept my story to myself, but I didn't. My grandfather told me that I needed to live life for more reasons than just myself. I wrote this book for many reasons beyond myself.

There was absolutely no way that I could fit my whole life story into this book without taking up about 10,000 pages. My life has been one heck of a ride. I didn't want to flood the audience with information overload. I also didn't want to leave anyone in suspense or "short-change" the audience or cheat them from the rest of the story.

So, I decided to break the book into a three-part series. This first book highlights the road I journeyed from my neighborhood in St. Louis to the life I have now. I wanted to tell the basis of the journey without being too long-winded. I wanted this book to capture the essence of my story and bring it to life.

Book Two will focus on the stories I didn't get to share with you. This includes my time in high school and college. Book Two will highlight the effects that PTSD, anxiety, deep depression, and abandonment had on my life. It will show how I made it out of those mental struggles and how I found light, love and peace in my life. Book Two will detail the road that led up to my writing *Reasons Beyond Myself.*

Book three will focus on my cousins from St. Louis and where they currently are in life. If you remember, I was given a way out of St. Louis, but my cousins couldn't leave. Book three will focus on their journeys in life, when they crossed paths with me, and where they ended up. It will look at their three lives in comparison with mine.

These three books together will provide an overall painting of the challenges and triumphs of life. Each book will connect together and create a special message, which we can all use to impact the lives of many.

I'm a cop, not a writer, so this has been a true learning process. I respect anyone who is able to tell an effective story to the masses, because it is a difficult process. Thank God, I was able to do it. I took my real life and put it onto the pages of a book. I did it for everyone reading this book. I want to share my story with the world, which in turn, opens the door for many other journeys in the life of others.

Thank you for reading and supporting this book! I know that as the reader you may have a million questions about the book, my job or just about me in general. The good news is that there are multiple ways to connect with me and my journey.

You can follow me on my social media platforms, which I will list below. I will be posting pictures in relation to the book and also have author/reader time where you'll be able to ask questions.

You can attend one of my seminars. I will be travelling across the nation to share my journey in person with my audience. Here, the audience will be able to hear about my journey firsthand and be able to interact with me more than just on the page. It will give more of an in-depth experience. I will be visiting many different locations and groups to speak about *Reasons Beyond Myself*.

Come to a book signing. Dates will be posted on my social media and my website.

At my events, I'll be addressing subject matters that weren't elaborated on in this book. I will also share updates on my immediate family that were mentioned in the book.

I will be traveling throughout Texas (and hopefully across the nation) promoting Reasons Beyond Myself. I hope to see you there!

Author Website: brionsimsjohnson.com

Instagram: @reasonsbeyondmyself

Once again, I thank all of you for your support and taking time to read this book. Share this book with as many people as you can. I appreciate all the support!

DEDICATION

This book is dedicated to the memory of my brother, Justin Tyrell Sims (1988-2021).